Cabin at Singing River

Building a Home in the Wilderness

Chris
Czajkowski

Foreword by
Peter
Gzowski

Camden House

Canadian Cataloguing in Publication Data

Czajkowski, Chris
    Cabin at Singing River

ISBN 0-921820-31-3

1. Frontier and pioneer life - British Columbia.
2. Wilderness areas - British Columbia.
3. Conservation of natural resources - British
Columbia. 4. Czajkowski, Chris. I. Title.

FC3828.1.C93A3 1991   971.1'04'092   C91-094360-5

F1088.C93A3 1991

To my team: Jack, Trudy, Lucky and Guenevere

Trade distribution by
Firefly Books
250 Sparks Avenue
Willowdale, Ontario
Canada M2H 2S4

Printed and bound in Canada by
D.W. Friesen & Sons Ltd.
Altona, Manitoba, for
Camden House Publishing
(a division of Telemedia Publishing Inc.)
7 Queen Victoria Road
Camden East, Ontario
K0K 1J0

Design by
Linda J. Menyes

Illustrations by
Chris Czajkowski

Front cover photograph by
Gary Fiegehen

Colour separations by
Hadwen Graphics
Ottawa, Ontario

Printed on acid-free paper

Acknowledgements

Much of this book was composed during the mid-1980s in the form of letters to Peter Gzowski's daily national radio programme, *Morningside*. I thank both Peter and CBC-Radio for inspiring me to launch myself into a new and exciting career as a writer.

I thank the Workers' Compensation Board for allowing me to use the extract from *The Fallers and Buckers Handbook*.

Thanks also to Katie Hayhurst, Dennis Kuch and their son Birch for their unfailing hospitality.

Special thanks to Trudy and Jack Turner, who gave me the chance of a lifetime and taught me much.

Contents

Foreword
by Peter Gzowski

I write this, as I write much of what I do away from CBC-Radio, in the refuge I still refer to as my "cottage," 50 miles from the nearest metropolis and perhaps a seven iron from the nearest store. I type my words on a Macintosh computer, remembering, as I do, the day an electrical storm blew out half a chapter of a book I was working on and left me helpless. On the deck outside my glass-walled study, two propane barbecues stand guard, their whipped-cream topping of snow evidence that we cooked indoors last night. Beyond them, cross-country skiers ply the tailored golf course, huffing and puffing under their woollen caps and diamond stockings, fashionably fit. I should join them but choose to write instead.

In the main room of the cottage, which opens off my study, Gill Howard, who shares my life, watches a British detective story on cable TV – the same screen where last night, over a soup we made from our store-bought New Year's ham, we chuckled over a video cassette from one of the five or six agencies that represent the newest and most profitable business boom in the local village. A fax machine sits beside the telephone – the tabletop receiver, that is, not the cordless phone I sometimes answer in the bathroom. Between sentences, I sip fresh coffee, the beans, now available at the local IGA, ground electrically, brewed in a machine and, if necessary, warmed in the microwave.

Ah, roughing it. We made this place ourselves five years ago, although making it, in our terms, meant getting my cousin Jack to oversee three Finnish carpenters and hire the electricians and the plumbers. I watched and opined. This is our nest, a retreat. My grandparents first came to this part of Ontario—Lake Simcoe country—after World War II. Theirs *was* a cottage—uninsulated clapboard around a stone fireplace, a rambling screened verandah, no electricity, no phone. Times change. Tonight, I'll check the weather channel on the cable to make sure I won't face freezing rain as I leave in my snow-tired BMW to make my return to city life.

Chris Czajkowski—it rhymes with the composer, in case you've never heard it on the radio—first wrote to *Morningside*, the CBC programme I host, in the season of 1984-85. Even by then, *Morningside* had begun to become what I've called "a village bulletin board of Canadian life." People wrote to it, as they still do, about all sorts of things, not only the issues of the day (and of the programme) but their own lives, their children, their pleasures—and sometimes their passions—and their troubles. Just before I heard from Chris, I had published an anthology of some of their letters, and its success had added to the already formidable amount of mail that now arrived on my desk every morning, as many as a hundred letters a day. Even in that avalanche, Chris's letter stood out: honest, unassuming, quietly lyrical and—I have long thought—quintessentially Canadian. We edited not a word. Jim Handman, a producer at the time, wrote a brief introduction; Lorna Jackson, one of the network's most experienced announcers, read it for broadcast. And so Chris and I began a one-way correspondence that, over the years, was to grow into one of the programme's most cherished regular departments—not to mention, as it turned out, to provide a seminal chapter in each of the subsequent editions of *The Morningside Papers*.

Quintessentially Canadian? We Canadians have, I think, mixed feelings about the landscape that surrounds us. On the one hand, we fear it; it is the enemy, as the school of literary criticism that has given us the *Wacousta* Syndrome (after the eponymous and vengeance-filled central character of one of our first novels) suggests. Northrop Frye makes the same point with his eloquently argued "garrison mentality," in which the garrison is our attempt to shield ourselves from the environment (and, as Frye contends, the landscape's original inhabitants), to turn our backs on the harsh natural world around us, to keep, at least in the earliest days, a little bit of Europe safe indoors from the raging snows. I do that now, cozy in my year-round country house. On the other hand, there is our fascination with the land; it is a character in much of our literature: W.O. Mitchell's prairies, Ernest Buckler's Nova Scotia farm, Farley Mowat's unforgiving North. The landscape is more than that too, more than just a literary symbol: it *is* us—

even at its rawest. Even for those of us who get there too seldom, the majesty of the North, our last frontier, lingers in our consciousness and helps to make us who we are. We are haunted by it. When Chris Czajkowski, British-born (as, indeed, were Susannah Moodie and Major John Richardson, who gave us *Wacousta* in the first place), and, on another level, Stephen Leacock, write about landscape, it strikes a chord with us.

I would not have expected to be so comfortable. As a boy, I played the wild games of Ernest Thompson Seton's *Two Little Savages*, earning "coups" that allowed me to dip the ends of sea-gull feathers in red dye and, on winter afternoons, mushing my chimerical dog team—"gee" for right, "haw" for left—along the sidewalks of Lansdowne Avenue in Galt, in southwestern Ontario. I would grow up to be a woodsman, I vowed, a trapper, living by my wits and my knowledge of the bush, reading the spoor of wild animals, at one with the elements. Now, half a century later, I wonder where the dream has gone.

Younger than I, the child of a Polish immigrant to England, Chris read many of the same books and, I take it, dreamed many of the same adventures. Cities never did seduce her. She studied agriculture, took off for Uganda first, then Australia and New Zealand, earning her living by milking cows and doing other people's chores, occasionally drawing and painting, happy with her own pursuits, seeking ever more remote corners of the world. When she got to Salmon Arm, British Columbia, she has said, she found it the most crowded place she'd ever been, and so she took off for the country she writes about in this book.

I met her—at last—in the spring of 1990. Her house was built by then, through the labours these pages describe, and she had taken some time off to come east, to talk with her publisher and to attend the National Magazine Awards, where a piece she'd published in *Harrowsmith* had garnered her a nomination. She came to the *Morningside* studio, where I introduced her to Lorna Jackson, her voice for so many years, and sat her down in front of a microphone. She was, I told her, almost exactly as I had pictured her: slim, fit, self-contained. She was happy to meet some of the people who had read her letters, but, the business of her eastern visit over, she was obviously anxious to get home. On the radio, I told her how much her reality echoed my own dreams and said that, even now, I could fantasize about changing places with her.

Would she like to host *Morningside* for a few days, I asked, while I went out to her valley and tried to live as I had once thought I would?

"Not for a moment," she said, and smiled her quiet smile.

PETER GZOWSKI
January 1991

Prologue

I t is April, and there is snow on the pass. I have been driving for many hours over ruts and mudholes, and it feels good now to drop from the cramped, stuffy cab of the pickup into the clean, sharp air. All around, the knobby hills and forest undulate in silence.

On a bluff by the side of the road is a barrage of signs. "Heckman Pass, 5,000 feet." "Steep Hill: Grades 18 percent." "Trucks check brakes here." "Chains MUST be carried at ALL times." "Avalanche Area: Do Not Stop."

Unlike me, the dog finds few messages in this unfrequented place; she is glad to climb back into the cab. She rests on top of a pile of equipment that brings her level with the windshield. There is no room for her in the back, for the old red truck is loaded with everything I own. I start the motor, and we begin the long grind down The Hill.

British Columbia

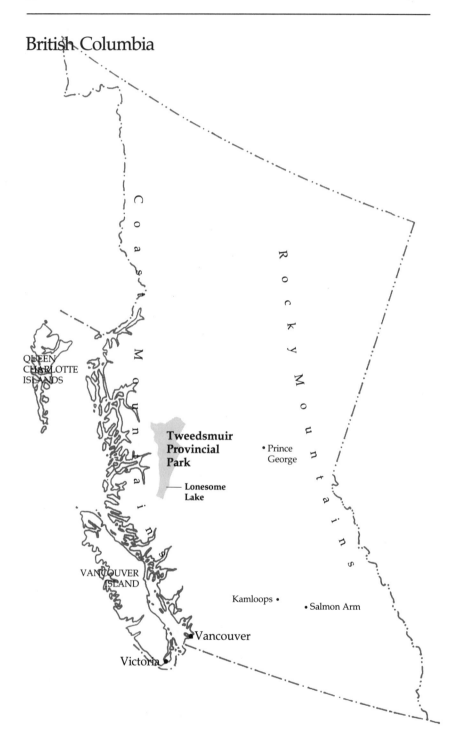

Chris Czajkowski's Cabin

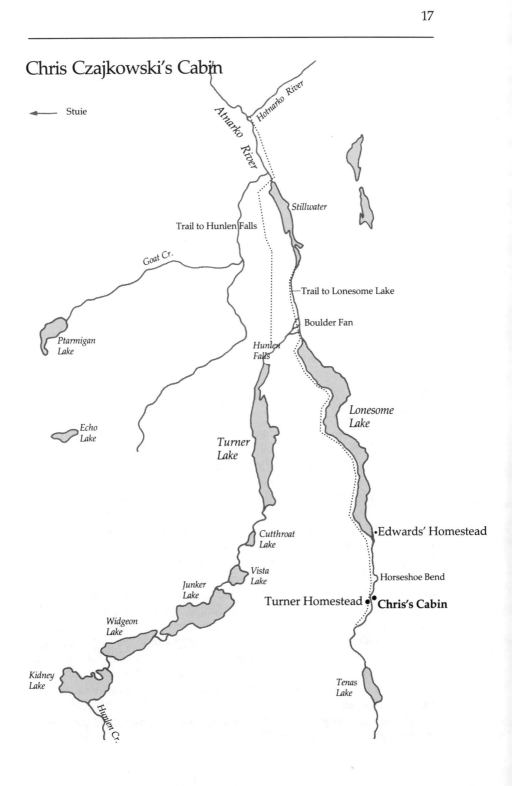

Stuie

Atnarko River

Hotnarko River

Stillwater

Trail to Hunlen Falls

Goat Cr.

Trail to Lonesome Lake

Boulder Fan

Ptarmigan Lake

Hunlen Falls

Lonesome Lake

Echo Lake

Turner Lake

Cutthroat Lake

•Edwards' Homestead

Vista Lake

Horseshoe Bend

Junker Lake

Turner Homestead •• Chris's Cabin

Widgeon Lake

Kidney Lake

Tenas Lake

Hunlen Cr.

Chapter 1

The Singing River

I sit by the singing river and watch the shallow water—quiet and a little drab at this "waiting" time of year—as it slides between mud banks and sandbars on its uneasy journey down the valley to the sea. It is not always as gentle as this, the river, but the snow and the winter cold still lock the surface water high in the surrounding mountains. Only the subterranean currents, which always flow, can seep through rock and glacier-milled gravel to emerge below the tree line and trickle down the steep, green, forested walls of the Atnarko Valley. Upstream from me, a small island, densely covered with birch and winter-grey alders, blocks the river and forces it into two complaining strands that run together into deeper water by my feet. On the far bank, three cottonwoods rise from a scribble of underbrush and clasp the hunched shoulders of a mountain, blank with snow, within the frame of their empty arms.

And I wonder, as so many of us do at turning points in our lives, whether I am doing the right thing. I have been offered a chance to build a cabin on this spot, 27 miles from the nearest road and 95 miles from a store, in the heart of British Columbia's Coast Range. A dream come true is staring me in the face, and I simply don't know if I can handle it.

Oddly enough, my childhood at the edge of a nondescript village in Britain fitted me quite well for the life that I now contemplate. My father was a wartime Polish refugee, and he started a business making furniture and restoring antiques. I played first with the thin, curled shavings swept into aromatic heaps beneath the benches and later with my father's tools. My mother, too, was very creative, and I soon learned that almost anything we wanted could be made.

My parents did not mix socially, and I was a loner. I spent thousands of hours exploring the uninhabited woods and fields behind the house, expeditions that evolved, as my horizons expanded, into two-week-long solitary hikes in the mountains of New Zealand, in the Andes and on the treeless, roadless, windblown grasslands of the Falkland Islands. Not that I am a hermit—far from it. I enjoy people, but I also enjoy being alone —not just alone in a room or for a few hours on a beach, but truly alone, days and miles from the nearest human being. It is a heady experience that stretches senses and intensifies thoughts. It is only then that I can be wholly myself.

I would not, however, be alone if I built my cabin here: indeed, without help, I would not know where to begin. Atnarko, according to an elder of the Bella Coola Indians, means "the place where the people are." It probably referred more to the lower parts of the river, which were used as a source of seasonal food and for cedar-bark harvesting, but it is appropriate for me too. Beyond the tangle of underbrush that spawned the three cottonwoods is a clearing of perhaps 20 acres, a wedge of tame grass running between the river and the abrupt walls of the forest. In it are a well-kept, steep-roofed barn, outbuildings and a neat, weathered log house. Both clearing and buildings are the handiwork of Jack and Trudy Turner, who have lived quietly here for 34 years.

Trudy Turner, née Edwards, has been in the area for much longer than that, though. She was raised two miles downriver, where the Atnarko opens out into Lonesome Lake, a long, S-shaped body of water named by her father when he preempted land for a homestead there in 1912. He had come by ship to Bella Coola, travelled up the valley to Firvale (where the road ended at the time), then followed the Atnarko River to the first unclaimed piece of land suitable for farming. Ralph Edwards was an ingenious man who saw no reason why he could not do what other men said was impossible. Among his many notable exploits was the construction of a water-driven sawmill almost 40 miles from the nearest road. Most remarkably, all his knowledge was obtained from books sent by mail to the nearest post office, then horse- or backpacked to his home.

Ralph married and had three children. The two sons worked outside for a while, but Trudy wanted nothing more than a place of her own. The nearest piece of land with any amount of soil was two miles upriver from her parents' place. She had built the claim cabin and started the clearing that would eventually give her title to the land by the time

Jack Turner traced her father's footsteps up the valley and walked, quite literally, into her life.

I flew into Lonesome Lake the first time I visited the Turners. I had been in Canada just two years and was milking cows on a commercial dairy farm near Salmon Arm, in southern British Columbia. My neighbours laughed when I said that the Salmon Arm area was too crowded. Many of them had come there from Vancouver and Calgary; to them, the town was laid-back and rural. But I had never lived in such a populated place: the unceasing roar from the Trans-Canada Highway, the mile-long trains that screeched and groaned up the gradient near the farm, the suburban sprawl that clogged the shores of Shuswap Lake in all directions. These were not what I had come to Canada for.

One day, I took out a road map of the province. A dotted yellow line, signifying a gravel road, ran westward for almost 300 miles from Williams Lake until it reached Bella Coola on the coast. Since there were very few place names along the road, it seemed an area worth investigating. By great good fortune, a neighbour in Salmon Arm knew the Turners. What is more, he had obtained for them a horse-drawn tedder, a machine for fluffing up hay to hasten its drying. (Until then, Jack and Trudy had turned all their hay by hand.) The only way to get the tedder to the Turners was to freight it up to Nimpo Lake, about two-thirds of the way along the dotted yellow line west of Williams Lake, and fly it into Lonesome Lake by floatplane. The tedder just fit into the back of my old ¾-ton pickup; in return for my trucking it up there, the Turners, with whom I was by then corresponding, offered me a ride in on the plane.

When driving west on Highway 20 from Williams Lake, one is hardly aware of the long, slow gain in altitude. The mountains, when they are visible, lie distantly and comfortably along the west and south horizons. Even as we flew toward them in the plane, skimming the ragged points of the lodgepole pines that carpet the interior plateau, the mountains did not seem to grow much. But suddenly, the ground fell away: the plane hung over a yawning chasm—a deep, north-south slash in the earth that sucked us down between plunging walls—then circled to lose height until we hissed down upon the quiet lake below.

I loved it, of course. I loved the giant coastal trees; the roaring, sparkling river; the soaring mountains; the flowers; the horse-powered haymaking (how much more pleasant than the fumy, rackety, backbreaking toil of tractor and baler I had worked with so often before); the drama of a summer storm; the wolverine swimming in the river (the only time I have ever seen one); and the hike down the valley out to the road.

After my second visit—I stayed in there alone for 10 days in winter, looking after the animals while the Turners went out on business—Jack and Trudy asked me if I would like to build on their property. To say I was dumbfounded would be an understatement. The Turners seemed so completely self-sufficient that I never dreamed they would want anyone else in the valley.

But times, and the river, had changed. The road, when it was pushed through to join Bella Coola with the rest of the province in the 1950s, veered away from the original horse trail and the Atnarko River. Other settlers in the upper valley, including Trudy's parents, had died or moved on, and no one had replaced them. One of the best pieces of land was drowned when Goat Creek went on a rampage in the fall flood of 1936, blocking the valley with boulders and creating a shallow lake where a stretch of natural hay meadows and three cabins had once stood. In 1956, the boundaries of Tweedsmuir Provincial Park were extended southward to encompass the Turners' property, irrevocably precluding any chance of closer habitation; and finally, their daughter Susan grew up and left home to make her own way in the world. So Jack and Trudy were farther from neighbours than they had ever been; they felt it would be wiser, in case of emergencies, to have a third person nearby.

The offer seemed too good to be true. Confronted with such an opportunity, I could not help asking myself if the reality would be as good as the dream. I went back to Salmon Arm, to the mundane world, to think about it. That was more than a year ago, and although I have been through the process of closing down my old life and preparing for the new, I am still not sure that I want to go ahead with it. There is still time to back out.

Chapter 2

The Decision

I would have left my gear at the floatplane base at Nimpo Lake, 50 miles from the top of The Hill, for most of it, like the tedder, will have to be flown in. But although the ice went out from Lonesome Lake in April, Nimpo Lake, which is much higher, is still frozen and will remain that way until well into May. Until then, the floatplane base will be closed. So my dog and I and all my worldly goods drove over Heckman Pass and down into the Bella Coola Valley.

Driving down The Hill seems, in some ways, not a lot different from flying, because little except empty space can be seen beyond the hood of a vehicle. This upstart goat track was built by local businessmen from settlements on both sides of the pass who volunteered the time and equipment to bulldoze it through after the government refused to do the job. The road hairpins slowly down the face of a cliff; although it has been vastly improved over the years, there are still grades as steep as 18 percent, many single-lane sections and a great deal of nothing beyond the crumbling, uneven edge. The road grinds down into the very bowels of the Earth; as it descends, mountain walls rise to shut out the expanse of sky. And in April, it is a journey through time as well, for at the top, snow buries the countryside and winter grips the silent, sparsely forested pass, but at the bottom, 4,000 feet below, it is spring.

Here, the road is submerged in trees. The air is redolent with the heavy scent of balsam, and craggy-armed firs and crinolined cedars stand red-trunked and massive beside the rocky, rushing Atnarko. Towering clouds form and break and form again about the peaks. Avalanches roar from teetering overhangs, and ribbons of foaming waterfalls froth and spout down sheer rock walls.

From the bottom of The Hill, the highway—sedate, two-laned and paved for its final 50 miles—continues west to Bella Coola. But I leave it and turn the laden truck onto a tote road, crashing and lurching as far as I can go—seven miles at this time of year. The river rolls and sparkles below the jolting vehicle, eagles swing against the crumbling cliffs above me, and mule deer spring through the broken fences of an abandoned homestead, leaving tufts of hair on the sagging, rusty wire.

The drive from the highway takes an hour, and it is a relief to exchange the numbing confines of the cab for the river-roaring wilderness. At last, I can feel the earth slowly and alone. I can savour the rough-barked trees and the bite of boot on rock. I can listen to the song of the river. I have been in many wildernesses, in many parts of the world. No matter how strange they are to me, I slide into their rhythms like a hand into an old glove. Their wonders and their intricacies make sense to me.

This is the route I shall normally use in and out of Lonesome Lake, for I don't plan on flying on a regular basis. I would like to come out at least once a month for mail. I hate flying, but there are many other reasons that make chartering a plane impractical. Expense is a major consideration: the money to fly in my freight will have to be found, but I certainly cannot shell out $100 a trip for me and my dog. Even flying one way and walking the other would not work. The shortest route between Lonesome Lake and Nimpo Lake is too wild and mountainous for foot travel; I will have to keep to the Atnarko Valley, and the place where it joins the road is 70 miles distant from the floatplane base.

My pack fits comfortably against the hollow of my back; the dog, a grizzled, shaggy, medium-sized mongrel, is overjoyed at the prospect of a walk. I cross a footbridge and start walking along a trail originally cut by Ralph Edwards but groomed by the provincial park staff. It will not serve me long, for it will soon climb out of the valley to take hikers to a spectacular view of one of the park's most dramatic features, Hunlen Falls. But I am able to follow it for three miles. It climbs easily up and over bluffs and down through dim stretches of cedar forest until it deposits me at the foot of the Stillwater.

This is the lake that was once a hay meadow. A sinuous line of bleached trunks and blackened stumps is all that is left of the cottonwoods that used to line the river. The settlers' trail was drowned along with the grass and the cabins; as the shores were steep, freight was pushed up the new lake on a raft. The horses and all their hay were similarly transported (for there was now no feed along this part of the journey); packing became such a laborious and time-consuming chore that the arrival of the floatplane base at Nimpo was hailed with relief. The Turners still have a boat there – they brought me down the lake in it the first time I visited them – but now I am alone and on foot. I have to scramble round the edge of the lake, balancing on rock slides and wading through swamps, while willows and wild roses claw at my face and pack.

Upstream from the Stillwater, the river splits and runs in braided skeins through dark stands of cedar, an Emily Carr landscape of green and gloom, a prime place for mosquitoes in the summer and grizzlies in the fall. Pale cottonwoods send vast, corrugated trunks into the canopy, and devil's club writhes like a mass of spiny snakes beside the boggy creeks. The remnants of the settlers' trail are visible in places, but it is rarely used and is no longer maintained. Great windfalls crisscross it in hopeless tangles, and much of the original route has been obliterated by the vagaries of the river. It ends abruptly in a deep, washed-out gully, still half a mile from the foot of Lonesome Lake, where it crosses the boulder fan below Hunlen Falls.

Hunlen Creek is a tributary of the Atnarko, born in a ring of mountains surrounding a high plateau to the west. It strings together a chain of seven lakes, slips quietly to the rim of the Atnarko, then leaps unbroken a thousand feet to atomize into veils of spray in the bottom of a deep, twisted canyon. Over the centuries, tons of rock have spewed from the canyon and dammed the Atnarko River, creating Lonesome Lake.

From the gully that has consumed the trail, I can see only the tip of the falls, a smooth, slim column of water that disappears mysteriously behind a buttress at the back of the canyon. The tourist lookout, the culmination of the park's trail on which I started my journey, is near the top of the falls. Few people have been to the bottom, for the creek, pounding between the sheer, contorted walls of the canyon, allows access only during the driest times of the year. However, once the creek erupts and spreads over the boulder fan, most of the water runs underground. In April, only a little trickles clear and clean over the shattered, speckled granite in the gully. But the enormous chaos of the next half-mile – the gaping washouts, the trees half-buried in drifts of boulders, the logs splintered and gouged by rocks and pounding water – proves that this gentle stream can swell with an awful fury that literally moves mountains. At every flood, it carves new channels and builds new barriers; the very ground shakes until the water subsides.

Picking my way through rock and eroded root, I come, quite suddenly, to the foot of Lonesome Lake. Like the Stillwater, it fills the narrow valley so that its steep, rocky shores plunge without a break beneath the water's surface. The day is ending: the sun has dropped behind the canyon, and the evening shadows have moved far up the eastern side of the valley.

I still have 10 miles to travel, 7 of them around the precipitous shoreline of Lonesome Lake. I know that there is a trail, but I have not seen it: when I journeyed through this valley before, the Turners brought me down the lake by boat. The trail was originally cleared for emergencies during freeze-up and break-up times, when the lake itself could not be travelled. A loaded horse could not manage the trail, but an unladen one might be coaxed along it, provided one carried an axe to cut out windfalls or to reroute the path around washouts. It will be hard to follow now, and as there do not appear to be any camping spots on the steeply sloping valley sides en route, it seems prudent to camp here, where wood, water and a safe place to build a fire are easy to find and where the smooth sheet of lake water narrows and slides over the first rocks of the boulder fan.

Sitting beside a cottonwood that is growing knee-deep in boulders, I watch the wind die and the water grow still. The fluted curves of a snow-covered mountain sail like a fully rigged ship at the head of the lake, shining gold, then orange, then pink with the last of the sun. The smoke from my small fire floats like a blue ghost into the silent branches of the trees. I unroll my sleeping bag and lie gazing at the stars while small creatures creep stealthily through the drifts of last year's leaves.

Along the bluffs and rugged places, the trail around Lonesome Lake is not too hard to find, for bears and moose keep it marked by their passage. (Indeed, Ralph Edwards, who built it, would have used existing animal trails wherever possible.) It is within the stretches of struggling forest, where old leaves and windfalls disguise it, that I lose the trail frequently and have to flounder through tangled brush and scramble over rock slides until I find it again. The last mile of the lake is a little easier, as I am now travelling round the lagoon, a stretch of weedy shallows almost cut off from the main part of Lonesome Lake by a band of willows running along the river channel. The foot of the lagoon is deepest, and it is here, at the crude pole wharf which the Turners built, that the plane will land with my freight.

Stepping onto the Turners' trail at the head of the lagoon is like driving from a bush road onto a four-lane highway. Two more miles, and the forest ends in a straggle of blackened stumps and a seven-foot-high fence of closely layered rails. The Turners built it around their property in an effort to discourage the deer that come down the mountains in spring to sample from the carefully nurtured hayfields. The clearing, won so painstakingly, is too precious to share with the wild creatures.

The house is easy to distinguish from the small cluster of weathered buildings, because it is the only one to sport a chimney. From it spouts an attendant puff of smoke. I push open the heavy pole gate, which screeches abominably on its homemade birch-fork hinges, and walk across the clearing to the house. I have travelled for a day and a half, walked 20 miles, and I am just in time for lunch.

So here I sit in the late afternoon, by the singing river, on a stump where perhaps my porch will be, watching the water, quiet and a little dull as it slides between the mud banks and sandbars. I left spring behind again as I came up the valley. Here the buds on the alders are clenched tight, and the day has lost its sparkle. I try to see a home behind me on the narrow shelf between the river and the valley wall, but the site is covered with giant firs, crisscrossed by lesser scrub and windfalls; it looks formidable. I have not built a house before, nor fallen a tree, and I have had very little experience with a chain saw. I know there will be difficulties I cannot yet imagine; the logistics of living so far from the road might be more than I can plan for. How will I move the logs across the ground? How will I lift them into place? How will I cope with living so far from the rest of the world? How will I get on with my neighbours? And how will I find the money to live?

I look at the Turners' tight log buildings across the river, at their steep-roofed barn, which is much higher than I would want to build my house. I think of the pioneers before me, who tackled this wilderness with far fewer resources than I have at my disposal. Here is the chance of a lifetime: I would be a fool to throw it away. If other people can do it, then so can I.

Chapter 3

Packing Home the Gear

A sudden roar, and the orange Beaver hops over the eastern rim of the valley. As it spirals down between the valley walls, I see a flash of green under its wing and know that my canoe is strapped to its float. I will need it to ferry freight to the head of the lagoon, but it will also make my trips up and down the valley much easier.

The plane carves a creamy wake across the lagoon and taxis to the wharf. As I lash its trailing ropes to the cleats, the pilot climbs onto the unladen float and begins to haul the heavy boxes of tools and food, pots and pans, tarps and drums of fuel out of the body of the plane, handing them to me one by one. Finally, he ducks under the propeller, unties the boat and flips it into the water with a smack.

Canoeing is something else that I have never done before, and the craft, which was so heavy and awkward when I had lugged it about on land, seems suddenly as light as a leaf, with a life of its own. The smallest of tugs brings it docilely to my feet. But a brisk wind has sprung from nowhere, and as the plane roars away, the little boat is dancing like a mayfly. Now how does one get into the thing without tipping it over? I pull it up against the wharf and tentatively stretch a foot into the bottom. Immediately, a large gap widens between my legs, and I leap back onto solid land. I try again with the same result. Surely I am not at fault. Can I blame the wind?

Feeling somewhat guilty—at the root of it all, I recognize plain and simple cowardice—I pull the canoe out of the water, load my pack with the tarp and a box of food and hike home.

The next day is a gem of spring-willow green and dew shine, and the lagoon is glassy. The spring runoff is close to its peak. The river and creeks are roaring and white, and the lagoon has risen a couple of feet since I was here in April. It creeps about the willow roots in the indented parts of the shoreline; the mats of slough grass are awash. I hear a faint splashing and squint across the water into the sun; on the far side of the lagoon, close to the willows that line the river, three moose feed, haloed in light against the indigo-shadowed mountain. Kicking up glittering shards of water, they wade through the shallows, strangely jointed, almost mechanical-looking creatures, relaxed and at ease with their environment. My heart gives a lurch of excitement: this is why I am here, to experience one of the few places on Earth where giant, wild creatures still roam free. What a privilege it is to be a part of the primal world.

I launch the canoe into the water, and it lies innocently by the wharf. I very cautiously extend my weight into it and settle onto my knees, mimicking an illustration I once saw in a book. I give the wharf a little shove, and upon severing that tie with the land, I am borne into a new and magical world I never knew existed.

One pull of the paddle sends the canoe sliding over the water. It is like flying, like hang gliding over the plummeting depths of the reflected mountain walls. My boat floats between the real and the upside-down worlds. Beneath the hull, patches of weeds swim up to meet me; in the shadows of their forests lurk needle-thin squawfish and suckers with gulping, vacuum-cleaner mouths. Suddenly, a breeze blanks out the mirror world, wavelets tinkle against the thin fibreglass hull of my boat, and beneath it, trembling sunlight flickers over the sandy bottom.

My dog, who has been yelping up and down the shore in panic (she treats anything remotely damp with the utmost horror), is enormously relieved at my safe return to the wharf. Upon being allowed into the bow, she promptly curls up and goes to sleep. What a soulless companion to have at a time of such revelation.

With the canoe, I transport all my freight from the wharf to the head of the lagoon, and the Turners bring Lucky down to help me pack it the rest of the way to the homestead. Lucky is a big brown horse with a stolid disposition and great hooves. He stands resignedly beside the piles of gear, the crosstrees of his pack saddle perched atop his bony back. The Turners drape him with ropes, heave up the sacks and boxes, then swathe the whole lot in a tarp.

We make a strange procession coming up from the lake. Jack goes first with a tall pink bale of fibreglass insulation bobbing on his packboard. Trudy is next. She carries a fat roll of green rubber foam and two yellow iron pieces of wheelbarrow that stick up behind her head like horns, giving her a decidedly snail-like profile. She leads Lucky with his lumpy load, and I take up the rear. My view is restricted to a pair of massive haunches and dinner-plate feet as the phlegmatic animal plods over the rocky trail, breaking wind frequently and copiously in my face. I carry four gallons of gasoline in a five-gallon can (fuel must always be carried by humans because it burns horses), and it is a most peculiar sensation. The liquid sloshes back and forth with its own rhythm, and I have to keep step with it or be thrown off balance.

Horse-packing the gear takes a couple of days; then, I begin to build a snug camp about 300 yards downriver from the house site, well out of the way of falling trees. A blue tarp, stretched over a frame of poles, covers the coffin-shaped rectangle of mosquito netting that encloses my sleeping bag. Winds can be fierce here, so it is too risky to have an open fire for cooking; the Turners have lent me an old, rusty tin camp stove, which reposes under one end of the awning, its chimney wired to a couple of birch trees. I store my food in a metal garbage can in the hope that it will be safe from squirrels, mice and weather; plates, pots and the water bucket are stacked upside down on a pole rack outside. I will have to scrounge the bush for poles and rails to make a fence around my little empire, because later, the cows will be let over to this side of the river to graze the rough, stump-filled meadow that surrounds me. As I well know from experience, they are the nosiest creatures in creation, and they would have a glorious time if let loose among my possessions.

The spring is often hot and dry in the Pacific Northwest – even Captain Cook complained of the light, balmy winds of May that hindered his final journey north – but this year, the season is wet. Walker's Dome, the mountain framed by the cottonwood trees across from my house site, has been invisible for several days; soft fingers of cloud ferret among its steep, shaggy-maned ridges. Water, dripping off the trees, plays a syncopated rhythm on the different surfaces of the camp: a plop as a drop hits the tarp; a splat in a puddle; a plink on the pots; a thwuk on the plastic water bucket. Plop, plop, plop; splat, thwuk; plop, plink, plop. The striped sparrows trill as they flit among the drooping alders on the bank, and the swollen summer river, the grey-green, rain-starred river, slides everlastingly by and fills my ears with its song.

Chapter 4

Considerations at the Base of a Tree

T he time has come when I can no longer put off using the chain saw. I hate machines. They stink, their noise drives me crazy, and their behaviour is idiosyncratic and illogical. I can grudgingly accept that they have to be fed, but when they don't start easily or run without a fault, they make me mad. This particular machine is also horribly dangerous. So it is with considerable apprehension that I place *The Fallers and Buckers Handbook* on an old log and open it to page 13. It begins, somewhat philosophically, with the title "Considerations at the Base of a Tree" and continues: "Falling a tree requires a great deal more consideration than merely bringing it to the ground.

1. Brush and debris adjacent to the tree shall be cleared away.
2. The tree must be assessed with regard to:
   (a) loose limbs
   (b) other trees that may be involved when the tree falls
   (c) lean, if any
   (d) the best escape route."

Then follow two nicely coloured diagrams of vertical pillars with wedges cut out of their perfectly parallel sides. A whole page of measurements in both centimetres and inches shows me how to make the correct cuts. I look at my jumble of wilderness. None of the trees resemble the diagrams, but one young fir, about 15 inches through, is leaning very obviously over a nice clear patch of ground. There is no close brush, and I can run in any direction. I look hard at the tree and try to imagine how the saw will cut it, pushing into the back of my mind the vivid illustrations of "Dutchmen" and "Barberchairs" and all the accidents that the book so explicitly pictures. Half the volume is devoted to fatalities, listing the numbers of widows and fatherless children and giving a graphic description of each demise.

The handbook also informs me that no one should attempt to fall a tree without an expert instructor alongside, but I can do very little about that. I put on my ear protectors and fire up the saw. It seems criminal to rip into the living flesh of the tree, but if I want a house, I will have to do it. The new chain bites cleanly, and in no time, a little wedge pops out. I move to the other side and begin the back cut, becoming very conscious of the massive weight, whose support I am so rapidly undermining, poised above me. The tree shakes, the back cut widens, and with a creak and a thump, the tree is on the ground. Well, that was easy. The tree is neither straight nor very thick and therefore useless for building, so I limb it and buck it up into stove lengths. How rapidly one can reduce 100 years of growth to firewood.

Emboldened by this success, I decide to tackle a big tree. The 26-inch bar of the saw will reach only a little over halfway through it. It does not lean much, but eventually, using an axe as a plumb line and squinting past it at the tree from every possible direction, I come to the conclusion that the tree will fall toward the river. I cut out the wedge, working from both sides of the tree, but before I finish the back cut, the tree shifts slowly in a direction opposite to the one I calculated. The bar is pinched tight. I switch off the saw and jerk at it, but with several tons of tree sitting on it, it is not going to budge. I survey my handiwork in horrified silence. This is the dreaded Dutchman. (Why on earth was it given that name?) I will have to go across the river to get some advice. "You did not allow for the weight of the branches," says Jack. "Notice how they're all growing on one side?" Did I not read the handbook properly? Surely it would have mentioned such an obvious piece of information. I scan the book again but can find no reference to branches. This is one lesson I will learn by experience alone.

I have another, smaller saw; the only solution is to make a second set of cuts above the first and in the opposite direction. But it is some time before I can pluck up the courage to do so. I visualize the tree squashing me like a beetle or the saw knocking into something as I try to run away, kicking back and ripping me in half with its greedy teeth. But finally, the tree comes down in a welter of broken branches and clouds of red dust, leaving me with plenty of time to shut off the saw and step out of the way. My nerves unwind slowly; the ensuing silence is a little creepy. A patch of sky has opened up above me; twigs and needles still sift down from neighbouring trees. A sapsucker, a small woodpecker with a vivid red helmet, zips into the clearing.

The fallen giant looks grotesque, belly up and defenceless. Its limbs are dense, massive, tangled and contorted; each will have to be bucked up into several pieces before it can be lifted. The trunk is far too thick for a house log. I cannot move it unaided, even bucked into the 13-foot lengths I shall use for lumber making. It will have to lie there until the horses are available. Because feed is in such short supply around the homestead, all the animals except Lucky are at this moment foraging in a wild meadow 15 miles upriver. They will not be fetched home until they are needed for hay-making in July. In the meantime, I must try to establish the area I will need for the house and a place to put the enormous brush piles that I will accumulate (burning is both dangerous and illegal at this time of year and cannot be done until the fall). The task is not as easy as it might seem, for until all the trees are out of the way, I cannot see what I am doing. Not only do I wish to design the house with the best possible view, but I also want to preserve several of the more interesting trees around it.

My routine over the next few weeks becomes a living nightmare. I have to steel myself to shatter each early-morning stillness with the maniacal scream of the chain saw. I am terrified of it. I struggle through half a dozen trees a day. The falling has to be done early, for the wind gets up in the afternoon; besides, the cows are now grazing this side of the river, and they cannot be let across the bridge after their morning milking until my daily quota of trees crashes earthward. Otherwise, the cows would inevitably investigate the situation at the worst possible time.

Most of the trees come down satisfactorily, but some fall into the welcoming embrace of their craggy-armed neighbours, and it is always an agony deciding what to do with them. "Never," cautions the handbook, "fall a third tree onto a second one if the second one is stuck." But the temptation to try it is strong, and I end up with an even worse mess. Usually, I chop lumps off the bottom of the miscreant's trunk until the trees part company and the cut one falls away; but occasionally, if another standing tree gives me good protection, I pick cautiously at the one against which the hung-up tree is leaning, ready to jump back like a shot, because this tree is now under considerable tension and it will come down with a rush.

Other trees are cut right through, but they still stand there, balancing on the hinge. If I cannot wedge them over, I give them a wide berth and wait until the wind brings them down. One tree is particularly difficult. I puzzle over it with a plumb line for days, and every time I look at it, I change my mind about its direction of fall. The top appears to be exactly above the bottom, and the branches seem evenly spaced all the way around. But its trunk twists and kinks along every inch of its 100-foot height. It is one of the last trees left in the clearing. I take a deep breath and

tackle it: it pirouettes on its stump like a ballet dancer and falls in a totally unexpected direction—fortunately, away from me.

I spend the rest of the day trimming branches, bucking the tree into lengths and piling the debris. My hands have grown tender ridges of calluses from the vibrations of the saw; they stiffen so painfully overnight that I can hardly bend my fingers in the morning. Every muscle in my body aches, and my legs are black with bruises where I bump into snags as I haul severed limbs to the brush piles.

The clearing looks like the aftermath of a holocaust. I am appalled at the destruction I have wrought. Huge stumps stick raw and jagged above the dismembered carcasses of trees that lie butchered into sections like the jointed backbones of some great prehistoric monster. The logs are so close together, I can cross from one side of the clearing to the other, like a squirrel, never touching my feet to the ground.

Most of the logs in the clearing are too thick for building (it would be a tremendous task to lift them onto the walls), and I have had to scour the property for trees that have a diameter of 12 to 15 inches. So many look perfect from one angle, but from another, they curve as gracefully as coconut palms—an artist's delight but a bane to a log builder. It is incredible that so much dense forest can yield so few straight trees.

What saves my sanity is a quiet loop of river we know as Horseshoe Bend, about half a mile below camp. The sweep of the river has thrown up a beach of white sand, where cottonwoods, toppled as the water washed the soil from their roots, lie with their ancient, bleached butts on the sand and their trunks in the clear, green water. I go there often to give the dog a run; she stays obediently in camp all day, away from the dangers of the chain saw and falling trees, and she is desperate for some attention and exercise.

The Bend is a marvellous, secretive place, hidden from the trail. How delightful it is to turn my back on the brutal destruction of the clearing and to leave behind the blackened stumps that stick out like rotten teeth in the Turners' cow pasture. There is no scrub beneath the cathedral firs in the untouched forest beyond the fence. Some of these trees are up to eight feet through. Where the sun penetrates the canopy and where enough moisture is retained by the thin skin of moss, needles and lichens that imperfectly covers the boulders, small flowers grow: the bold, white stars of the creeping dogwood; the tiny, shell-pink, scented bells of the twinflower; the sarsaparilla, whose stems are so thin that the mat of broad leaves seems to float like a magic carpet above the ground; and, most precious of all, the fairylike calypso orchid, whose shy magenta face bows toward the shadowy forest floor.

Occasionally, it is too hot to work, and I go to the Bend when the sun still shines and the ripples waver over the green depths. Glittering flecks of mica tumble slowly in the eddies. I fling off my clothes and stand in the icy flow while sculpins pounce at my toes, until the irritation of the flies on my bare skin is worse than the shock of the cold. I duck down and emerge, gasping, much to the bewilderment of the dog. Then how glorious it is to shoot downstream in the clean, cool water, swift as an otter, and stand and dry in the wind until the flies find me again, forcing me to pull on scratchy clothes and hot, heavy boots.

Most often, however, I work until the sun has dropped behind the mountain and I simply cannot push my aching body anymore. The soothing rhythm of putting one foot in front of the other unwinds my muscles and eases my mind. Down at the Bend, kingfishers chirr like English football rattles, and the silky current whispers as it coils palely in the evening light. The river there is fringed with willows much pruned by beavers. They do not attempt to dam the river but build lodges of chewed poles on the far bank. Their tracks are thick by the edge of the water, both paw marks and the stiff slashes of dragged branches, but although I have sat there for many an evening, I have never seen one.

Chapter 5

The Mail Run

Approximately once a month, I go down the valley for mail; each trip along the river is different. At the end of May, during the spring runoff, the boulder fan below Hunlen Falls is an uninterrupted froth of white water. It is impossible to remain dry-shod while hiking through. The deeper gullies have to be crossed on thin foot-logs slick with spray. It requires a concentrated effort to look only at the log and not at the dizzy maelstrom that pounds in every conceivable direction underneath.

The canoe on Lonesome Lake makes the journey to the road both faster and less strenuous, and although I always carry equipment with me, I do not often need to camp. Unfortunately, when I came in to start building my cabin, I could not leave my vehicle where I had parked it on my first trip up the river, because every year, the high water carves a washout on the tote road, rendering it undrivable for several weeks. The safest place to leave the truck is at Stuie, the first permanent settlement down the valley, 12 miles from the bottom of The Hill. So my first trip out would be farther than usual.

Stuie, a traditional native fishing ground, has a spectacular setting. It is overhung by the glaciated walls of three major mountains between whose shoulders crouch countless peaks, many unclimbed and unnamed. The present settlement owes its existence solely to tourism, although that part of the river is still used by the Carrier Indians during the summer salmon run. Two families live here year-round: the Corboulds, who operate a fishing lodge, and Katie Hayhurst and Dennis Kuch, who have developed a wilderness education centre for hikers and naturalists. I store my truck and town clothes with Katie and Dennis; they pick up my mail and sometimes find time to drive part of the way to meet me, although I often manage to hitch a ride despite the very infrequent traffic. It would be impossible to collect mail or visit the store without overnighting somewhere, so I feel very fortunate in having my Stuie neighbours. It would be a lot less convenient, and certainly less pleasurable, to conduct my outside business without them.

Needless to say, I am not yet very expert at planning all my purchases ahead, and there is usually something I want from the store. This involves a 30-mile trip farther down the river—swollen just below Stuie by the milky, glacier-fed Talchako and called, after the confluence, the Bella Coola River—to Hagensborg, 10 miles from the end of the highway, or to the town of Bella Coola, situated where the road finally meets the sea. The whole 50-mile stretch of valley, from the bottom of The Hill to the salt chuck, boasts no more than half a dozen stores, a couple of gas stations and hotels, a hospital, a small but excellent library, a Credit Union and the best homemade lemon pies in British Columbia, freshly baked at the Co-op coffee bar on Tuesdays, Thursdays and Saturdays.

One-third of the 2,000 inhabitants of the valley are native. Many of the original white settlers were Norwegian; their descendants provide the more conservative element of the population. The rest are a mixed bag. Most people have come here because the valley is beautiful; they stay because they like the community.

A lot has been written about the friendliness of isolated areas, and I have found the Bella Coola Valley no exception. However, city folk generally have a romantic notion about such places. They are astounded when people in the bush have disagreements that can sometimes lead to bitter and irreconcilable hatreds. They forget that those of us who live out here are also human. In cities, people are forced to ignore each other to survive; here, because of the distances between them, people are very much aware of their neighbours. The more aware one is of a person, the stronger the emotional involvement. Usually the involvement manifests itself as respect and affection, but it may work the other way. I know of siblings who own adjacent properties 20 miles from the next inhabitant, yet for years, they have not spoken to each other or let each other cross their land. This might seem incomprehensible to an outsider, but it is not the only such situation in the area. Yet despite these feuds, there is a strong undercurrent of loyalty: a neighbour would not hesitate to help a lifelong rival in a real emergency.

A trip to town is an event, and although I would not want to live down there, I look forward to my sporadic socializing. Almost before I step out of the truck, friends hail me, saying, "I heard you were down." It never ceases to amaze and amuse me how word gets around so quickly. City folk complain that this is an invasion of their privacy, and it makes them uncomfortable. But I like it that way: I feel as if I belong.

By the end of June, when I go out for my second mail trip, the big flush of the spring runoff has subsided and travelling conditions have changed again. The water is still fairly high, although no longer a problem, and at the beginning, I make good time. But on the way home, as I cross the boulder fan below Hunlen Falls and emerge from the forest by the outlet of Lonesome Lake, a wild, southerly wind slams into me, driving four-foot waves onto the stony beach where I usually launch the canoe. The boat will be smashed to pulp if I attempt to put it into the water. The wind is cold, but when I seek shelter from it, the mosquitoes bite with a fury. It is too wild and unsafe to light a fire, so I huddle in my sleeping bag, half stupefied with the roar of wind and water, and wait.

At last, a feeble sun breaks through the clouds. The shadows are already across the lake and partway up the eastern slope of the mountains. The wind drops fast, as it often does when the sun disappears from the valley, and the waves subside at once. Apprehensively, I push the canoe into the water, which is still fairly rough, but I need not have worried: even before I paddle past the first point, the lake has grown dead calm. The light soon dies from the sky, and stars begin to prick holes in the dusk. There is no moon. The darkness gathers until I can only dimly perceive the amorphous landmasses beside me blocking the stars. Nighthawks beerk as they slice the air with scimitar wings. As the lake becomes motionless, the stars are mirrored in the water. My craft becomes a spaceship, sliding over the black abyss of infinity, pushing aside the constellations with the slow swell of its wake. Bats flicker like black flames around an aura that encases me and my boat. Once, a loon calls, invisible, and so close that my heart stops.

I sleep beside the lagoon and finish the journey in daylight.

Chapter 6

July

The last tree is down! I have been a slave to the screaming saw for six long weeks. I can hardly believe that the torture has finally ended. I cannot look at a tree without sizing it up as a building log; I am even doing it in my sleep. I have a permanent crick in my neck from staring up into the forest's canopy, trying to decide if a suitable length might be extracted from a tree too wide or too twisted at the bottom. When I worked in the Falkland Islands, a fellow wildlife enthusiast and I once spent 10 days hiking round the incredible seabird colonies there. We took little food with us but lived on fish, wild goslings and greens. We were amazed at how rapidly our attitudes toward wildlife changed—as soon as we saw a movement, our first thought was not "How interesting" or "How exciting" but "Can we eat it?" Now I am that way with the forest. Will I ever be able to look at a tree with pure enjoyment again?

The next job is to peel the logs. Fir has a bark that is one of the toughest to remove, and I had hoped that the rising sap of spring and early summer would loosen it. But although the resin is plentiful and coats my tools and clothes so thoroughly that they stick uncomfortably to my skin, few logs peel easily. I chip and lever at them with an axe until they lie pale and naked, glistening in the intermittent rain. I have raised a new crop of blisters on my hands and have discovered, by their aching, yet more mus-

cles that I did not know existed. But this work is quiet, mindless and safe, and I can relax. Sometimes, Trudy and her daughter Susan, who is visiting for a while, come over to help.

It is the beginning of July; the Turners have been up to the horses' summer grazing ground and brought home a companion for Lucky so that when the weather cooperates, they can start the hay. On the more promising mornings, the clatter of the mower comes over the river with the smell of bruised and curing grass. If the weather stays settled, the next sound is the whirr of the tedder, the machine that I trucked to Nimpo from Salmon Arm. Its chicken-foot tines scratch the wilted grass apart, and when it is dry enough, the rake follows, clanging with the snap of a portcullis as it pushes the hay into heaps.

In the evening, when the sun drops below the rim of the valley and the blackflies bite less intensely, the horses are harnessed to the wagon that was an antique even when the Turners bought it 30 years ago. The wheels are so battered and shrunken that the iron tires do not fit anymore; they are lashed on with strips of rawhide that still sprout black, red and white hair.

Hauling hay can be accomplished more quickly with a third person, so if Susan is not there, I sometimes go over and help, particularly when the weather threatens. Lucky's companion is a bay mare called Guenevere, who, despite her age and gentle temperament, fancies herself a circus horse in harness. They make an oddly matched pair—Lucky with his deliberations and Guenevere with her prancing—but Trudy handles them with patience and skill. The old springless wagon groans and creaks as it lurches over the uneven ground between the haycocks.

Jack and I fork up the loose, slippery heaps smelling of crushed wild peppermint, one of the many herbs and weeds that grow among the handsown timothy and orchard grass. Trudy organizes the load and periodically lays ropes along its length. These will be tied together around a huge bundle of hay to form slings that will greatly assist the unloading of the wagon. The harness jingles as the horses shake their heads in an attempt to dislodge mosquitoes and horseflies or snatch at tempting mouthfuls of hay from the next raked heap. As the level in the wagon grows higher, the silvery harvest rustles like silk and scratchy bits fall down our necks.

The full load wallows like a ship toward the barn and stops outside the west gable end. The horses are unhitched, and one of them is harnessed to a long rope that runs over a pulley high up under the ridge of the roof. The other end of the rope is attached to the top slingful of hay; as the horse is coaxed forward, the sling sways up and into the barn, emptying the wagon in no time. Hundreds of swallows scream back and forth from their mud nests beneath the roof; the cats lick their lips and hope the hay will soon rise high enough to bring the baby birds within reach.

When they can spare the time, the Turners and their team come to my side of the river to do my heavy work. First, we clear the building site of the logs I have been unable to move myself and make roadways through the rest of the debris. Then a huge, solid, rock-scarred sledge made of thick birch timbers is harnessed to the horses and dragged to the places where I have unearthed stones that will become the cabin's foundation. This country of granite-fold mountains is all rocks, but few have anything resembling flat sides; I have spent long hours with a peavey – a long pole with a clawlike hook on one end designed for levering and rolling logs – hunting for well-shaped stones and grubbing them up from beneath the thin, green moss. We manoeuvre them aboard the stoneboat and lash them on with a heavy chain, then the horses throw themselves against their collars, leaping ahead until the sledge slews and grates and the runners smoke with friction. Clouds of dust boil behind, for despite the frequent rain, the thin soil dries immediately in the strong spring winds.

At last, I am ready to begin the actual building of the house. I started work on the clearing at the end of May, and it has taken me more than two months to reach this stage. I seem to have been working forever with very little to show for it, but suddenly, things are beginning to fall into place.

All the time I have been falling and bucking, dragging and peeling, I have been giving a lot of thought to the shape, size and location of my future home. I want space to weave and paint, I want as much natural light as possible, and I want to be able to see out in every direction. Naturally, such considerations as heat efficiency and snow load also have to be thought about. To accommodate all these things, I have decided on an L-shaped plan. I have also tried to position the cabin so that I can see the tip of Walker's Dome between the branches of the three cottonwoods across the river, for I love to watch the sunrise change colour as it works its way up from the summit of the mountain.

Essentially, the house is a 28-by-26-foot rectangle with an 8-by-13-foot notch cut out of the southwest corner. There will be four foundation logs, each 34 feet long; they will run east-west, parallel to each other and spaced equally across the 28-foot side, extending 8 feet beyond the 26-foot side to create a deck that faces west toward the river and the setting sun. Because of their length, each foundation log needs at least three supporting rocks underneath. Once the boulders are dragged onto the site, I roll and lever them into place. Then the stoneboat is unhitched, and the horses are led to the first foundation log. It is 18 inches thick at the butt and, even with the bark off, a big load for the horses. I have cut the sharp edges off the ends so that they will ride more easily over the stumps and rocks.

Trudy manoeuvres the team into position, and I fumble the awkward chain into loops about the end of the log, ever conscious of Lucky's feet so close to my head. "Giddap," says Trudy, and they are off. Guenevere flings herself against her collar and rebounds; Lucky slowly leans forward to take up the slack. Somehow, the unlikely pair pulls together, and the log leaps and snakes through the forest, its great tail whiplashing around stumps, giving Trudy an excuse for some very nimble footwork as she jumps from side to side with the reins. The dust rises and bars the sunlight, and the great log comes to a halt with its tip pointing toward the river. "Just a little bit," says Trudy. The horses jerk another step, and the log shifts a foot. "Back," she says, and the chain is slackened so that I can wrestle with the stiff, linked knots. The chain has bitten teeth marks around the neck of the log, and it has been well polished by its tumultuous ride.

At last, all four foundation logs lie side by side, scratched by stone and scuffed by dirt, butts toward the valley wall and tips toward the river. A friend of mine is staying with me, a man from Europe whom I met years ago in New Zealand. I put him to work as I notch each of the foundation logs so that they sit firmly on their rocks. The support in the middle complicates the fit, so we must cut, roll and check, then roll back and cut some more. But finally, the foundations are finished, and the logs lie 7½ feet apart, like a neat row of giant's pencils. It is an exciting moment. There is order among the chaos: something positive, at last, in the midst of all that destruction. I perch on the end of a foundation log and watch the sun sparkling off the singing river. I have come a long way since I sat here last April. I try to recall the clearing as it was then, with the uncut trees and the tangle of windfalls, but I find it difficult to remember. I can, however, quite clearly see a vision of my future home. At last, the cabin is begun.

Chapter 7

Hiking the Hunlen Chain

Like most people, I am mystified when the things that move me have little effect on others. My European Friend has expressed a desire to "live with nature and to go where there is no one else," and as he has travelled to 80 countries and hiked in all the major mountain ranges of the world, I have planned an exciting 10-day trip for us. I have not travelled most of the surrounding area, and I can hardly wait to explore.

E.F. is a linguist who teaches English and works as a translator. He is a slim, dapper man, proud of his appearance and physical fitness. Although he is obviously unaccustomed to using tools, he is certainly strong, for he has thrown himself into the work of the past few days with a great deal of vigour and coordination. He has black hair, very dark eyes and fierce eyebrows that end in little wings. A neat goatee emphasizes the angularity of his face. Every morning, he trims his chin with a bulky battery-powered shaver, and I have had a very hard time persuading him to leave it, and about 15 pounds of gear, behind. I am dubious about his light, crêpe-soled boots, but he insists that nowadays, every hiker wears them. His pack, which is frameless and looks very impressive with a plethora of pockets and straps and which puts my own oil-stained, homemade canvas sack to shame, is the latest thing in Europe. Every serious outdoorsman carries one. Perhaps the boots and the pack are stronger than they look.

E.F. is not an early riser. How can anyone who revels in the beauties of nature fail to leap out of bed at the first ring of the varied thrush while the blue dawn creeps into the world? What greater joy can there be than to watch the transition from shadow to sunlight, when the dew trembles in the windless hush and the mule deer, elfin and bold, pick a slender-legged path through the forest? Who could bear to miss the freshness of a golden morning, that fleeting light that fades so quickly as the day becomes worn and tarnished? E.F. can, it seems. He prefers to stay in bed.

So the sun has been up for several hours when we hike down to the lagoon and follow an abandoned surveyor's trail from the head of the lagoon toward the Hunlen lake chain. We have a steep climb of about 2,500 feet. The trail is well blazed, but it has not been maintained for years and it is thick with windfalls. The rocky valley side is sparsely treed here, mostly with lodgepole pine and young fir, legacy of a forest fire perhaps a hundred years ago. Pine is always the first to grow after a burn. It will be centuries before a mature fir forest can evolve; when it does, it will crowd out the smaller pines. Because we are so late, the sun glares full upon us, and we are both glad to reach a little, icy spring at the top.

The vegetation has changed. Lodgepole still dominates, but the underbrush is strange: slide alder, azalea, heather and crowberry and the short, shrubby Labrador tea that releases its spicy scent as we wade through it. The wind sounds different in this lighter, thinner forest. The country is very quiet, because we are out of earshot of the Atnarko and there is no moving water up here. Large stretches of bog provide breeding grounds for mosquitoes, and in one, a lesser yellowlegs has nested. It drives us away with its strident screams.

The walking is easy, and I expect to reach our destination within four or five hours of leaving home. But E.F. suddenly gives a great groan and flings himself down, complaining about the pain in his shoulders. We each carry about 40 pounds, and I am rather surprised that a hiker with Himalayan experience—not to mention the latest pack from Europe—should have so much trouble.

We struggle on, with frequent rests, and eventually emerge from the forest at Junker Lake. The view, hidden until the last moment by the trees, is totally unexpected. At the head of the five-mile lake, three 10,000-foot mountains soar into a shining sky. Triple-peaked Mount Talchako we can identify, but the names of the rest are unknown to us, for they are beyond the edges of our maps. A grey, sandy beach runs along the northeast shore of the lake, and here, warmed by the low evening sun, we make camp. E.F. has a small tent. He professes to be unable to sleep on hard ground, and he stretches his body first on sand, then on duff and, finally, on a piece of bog to find the softest possible bed. That it is damp and windless does not bother him. I prefer to lie in the open on the sandy beach, where the breeze dispels the flies and where I can track the satellites as they wink their way mysteriously across the shimmering sky. All night, small waves slop onto the beach, and the breakfast tea water is full of grit. I have drunk the first pot and am well into the second before E.F. crawls out from his little bog. His dapper mask has slipped a little: I do not ask him how he has slept.

From here on, there is no trail. The pines end, and older, wetter, much denser spruce forest spreads before us. Yesterday, we travelled a circular route, and we are now on the far side of Walker's Dome, the mountain that looms above my house behind the cottonwood trees across the river.

The bush is not too bad at first, but as we climb higher, the mountains grow steeper and the vegetation becomes shorter, tougher and much thicker. Progress is now hard work. "Find the fallen trees and walk along them," says E.F. "That is what we did in the jungles of Brazil." So we scramble and pant and swim through chest-deep azaleas smelling of skunk. I wonder, as I so often do at these times, whether such endurance tests are worth it. Suddenly, we find ourselves perched above the world in a long, sloping meadow starred with purple daisies. Far below is Junker Lake, blue and wind-roughened, the beach where we camped a pale rind at one end. The rest of the Hunlen lake chain strings out on either side of it like a necklace. We can see to the end of the high, mountain-ringed plateau and make out the little nick through which Hunlen Falls leaps into oblivion. In the other direction are the mountains that reigned so impressively over the campsite last night; they are now almost insignificant in a great panorama of rock and ice. The emergence from the bush has put springs into my legs. I have forgotten all weariness, and I grin delightedly at E.F. Surely, this is a perfect reward for all our efforts.

"But the flies," he wails. His face registers such black misery that he looks ready to weep. True, the horseflies are abominable. Huge and sluggish, they descend upon us in swarms. Even their startlingly beautiful emerald eyes cannot endear them to us. Their sharp feet prickle our skin, and they crawl in our hair, buzzing and rubbing our nerves ragged. It is hard to suppress the desire to flail our arms in a frenzy to drive them away. They are easy to kill, but it is so unpleasant to feel their juicy bodies crush beneath our fingers that in the end, we let them alone and pull raincoats and hoods tightly over our heads in an effort to shut them out. For me, the euphoria of being in alpine country more than compensates for this discomfort; E.F.'s miserable face elicits little sympathy.

The map shows a small lake farther round the mountain, which I hope to reach before dark. We start over a wide, shallow, stable rock slide, and with no bush to hinder us and the panorama to beckon us, it seems as though I stride over the boulders in seven-league boots.

"Argh," E.F. complains. "These rocks move. If I break a leg here, it will be impossible to get me out." His stylish boots give him little support. It is gradually dawning on me that this man, with his vast experience of the Swiss Alps, New Zealand Alps, the Himalayas and the Andes, not to mention the jungles of Brazil, has never been off a trail. His roughest trips have been with guides and porters who carried his baggage, and his impressive pack has been used only between the airport and the train station. He tells me that he would love to bring his friends to Canada on hiking tours, but we would have to find locals to carry their bags.

We hit tongues of dwarf pine and fir that slow us periodically, and it is a nuisance to walk in hooded raincoats in such hot weather, but I leave E.F. and his grumbles behind and round the skirt of the mountain. Framed by an exquisite grove of twisted pines, straight out of a Japanese brush painting, is the little lake. It has almost silted up and is full of reeds, but the turquoise water, opaque with glacial flour, is a perfect foil to the blooms of the blood-red Indian paintbrush. Behind the lake, a curtain of ice, old and snowless, seamed and cracked, hangs on a black mountain wall. Surely, this will cheer up my doleful friend.

"It's the lake," I call back to him. "The lake."

"Thank God," he says as he plods up to the little grove of Japanese pines. He looks for a long moment at the mountain, the snow, the flowers and the milky green swamp and exclaims, "But it has no water in it!" He tramps down into the basin in a gloomy rage and throws himself onto the ground. Instantly, he is writhing as the horseflies zoom in again.

There is a small rise of ground by the creek outlet that catches the wind and gives us a magnificent view of the mountains and the westering sun. The breeze helps dispel the flies, and soon, even E.F. can manage a wry chuckle at the thought of dressing in full rain gear on such a hot, sunny day. The horseflies disappear with the sun, and it is the last we will see of them. Why they should be so concentrated on that one day remains a mystery.

I sleep on the rise of ground by the creek, and E.F. zips himself into his private little bog. The next morning, we climb the spur behind the camp, aiming for the summit of Walker's Dome. There are no flies, we carry no packs, and there are no complaints.

It is an easy walk. As we climb higher, the ridge narrows and we can look back toward the lake chain. But we cannot see it, for the valleys are filled with a fog that laps at the foot of the mountain and maroons us; we are castaways in a sea of cloud. We pass patches of snow, and in sheltered places along the stony ground, jewel-like flowers cling to the hollows: starry saxifrages, porcelain-pink cushions of moss campion and the stalkless lapis-lazuli bells of campanula. Hidden trickles of water whisper hollowly underground, and small rocks, loosened by the sun, clunk occasionally down the worn wall of ice.

We reach a rocky peak, and the view is breathtaking. Vast abstract

sweeps of black rock and blinding snow swing hard-edged against an ultramarine sky. An icefield swoops down toward the lake chain, from which the fog is lifting in ethereal columns. The lakes float as in a dream. Range after range of mountains pulls us into the distance: the pinkish, volcanic Rainbows to the east and the endless vista of glacier-swathed peaks of the Coast Range to the west, stretching north to Alaska and 300 miles south to Vancouver.

There is something very precious about a still day high in the mountains. There is a barely discernible hum, perhaps merely the murmurings of distant wind and water, but I like to think of it as the sounds of the turning of the Earth:

And Holy silence bursts the ears:
Hush! The music of the spheres.

There is a little chirp, and my mind jumps instantly from the abstracts of infinity to the ground between my feet. In a crack in a rock sits a chipmunk. How on earth can he find enough to live on up here? The plants are scattered and the water far underground. He – and presumably there is a she too – must sleep most of the year. He flicks his wisp of a tail and disappears. We place a couple of peanuts by his perch. Such large seeds will surely be a feast in the chipmunks' miniature world: they are a fitting offering to the gods of the mountain.

The summit is still ahead of us. The view, when we scramble up to it, is not as spectacular as I thought it might be, for most of the Coast Range behind us is hidden by the chipmunks' peak. But east of the summit is the abrupt, 1,000-foot cliff face visible from the cabin site, and from it, we can see 7,000 feet straight down into the Atnarko Valley. Lonesome Lake, joined to the Stillwater by the thread of the river, wriggles like a worm. The Turners' homestead is nothing more than a smudged thumbprint in a vast, coniferous sea. Had we not known it was there, we would have missed it. Details are lost; even the sloping roof of the big barn is only a tiny dot. I can distinguish the scars of my clearing, however, for they stand out raw and yellow against the green.

E.F. has a pair of wonderful German binoculars. Very light, they fit easily into a pocket, but they are also very powerful. As soon as I see them, I covet them. As I bring them to my eyes, distances leap toward me and a world of patterns and details that I have never imagined is revealed to me. It is useless to think about owning such glasses, for the cabin must take priority over everything else; I have no money to spare for luxuries.

Sitting on the edge of the crumbling drop, E.F. focuses the binoculars toward the homestead. He stares reflectively for a long time through the lenses. "Hmm," he muses. "That second foundation log is definitely not straight."

We have several days of glorious weather and fabulous hiking. Sometimes the mosquitoes are a nuisance or the bush is thick: at one point, after a particularly frustrating struggle through a dense patch of spruce, E.F. says, "Now I know I can do anything." But mostly we keep in easier country along the fringes of the alpine, crossing successions of basins with gemlike lakes backed by tumbling glaciers. I am always excited by the strangely shaped, glistening ice with its blue and green crevasses, but E.F. has recently been to the Columbia Icefield in the Rockies, the biggest in Canada, and he is not so impressed.

Often we wade through acres of flowers whose brilliance and careless beauty no gardener can hope to emulate: paintbrushes from white to deep red, the scented spires of the white bog orchid, purple pentstemons and golden senecios, and the mauve daisies that seemingly retain the daylight after the sun has gone and gleam strangely in the dusk. Many others I cannot begin to identify. They grow in a riot of colourful and orderly profusion, grouped around bogs, rills, pools and tinkling waterfalls. But as I wax enthusiastic about the glories of the flowers, E.F.'s mind dwells elsewhere. He has an aversion to wet feet that is equalled only by my dog's. He spends an inordinate amount of time and energy keeping his boots dry.

One day, as we pick our way down a loose rock slide, E.F. shouts hoarsely, "A bear! A bear!" Sure enough, a grizzly is prowling beside an alpine pool. He can smell us, for his nose is up and questing, and as soon as he is sure of our direction, he gallops away and is quickly out of sight.

On the far side of the basin is a steep snow slab, and we have to make quite a detour to get around it. We are on a day hike, and later, when we return the same way, we find grizzly tracks leading straight down the snow slab. E.F., an expert skier, thinks he will follow them rather than make the detour again. Unlike me, he has no fear of steep snow slopes; even when the bear's tracks turn back, he continues. I am having none of it and go the long way around. E.F.'s head drops lower and lower, then suddenly he slips and hurtles out of sight toward the broken rocks at the bottom. There is an agonized wail, then silence.

It takes me some time to scramble to where he has fallen. He is quite unhurt. He has landed on sloppy mud, on the only soft bit of ground between jagged rock teeth at the bottom of the snow slope. He is wailing because he has, at last, got wet feet.

We slowly circle the chain of lakes and begin to head homeward on the south side of the plateau. There is less snow and ice in these basins, for they are more exposed to the sun. The flower meadows are extensive, and the whole mountainside is full of marmots. These fat, loose-skinned, dumpy creatures live on lupin roots and sleep for seven months of the year. Grizzlies consider them a feast and sometimes dig up great areas looking for them, but marmots' burrows are contorted and intricate, and their eyesight is excellent. There is always one sitting at a lookout; its piercing shriek, like a bosun's whistle, warns its comrades for miles around. These little sentries never fail to notice us, and we feel like visiting sea captains being ceremoniously piped around the mountain.

On the ninth day of our hike, we suddenly come upon boot prints, the first sign of other humans that we have seen since we climbed out of the Atnarko Valley. We have arrived at the foot of the lake chain. We drop down through the tree line and make for the campground at the head of the park's trail, which leads up from the tote road. I will leave E.F. here, for the trail is well marked and he will have no trouble finding his own way out to the highway. The campground is deserted. We drop our packs and hike the last half-mile to the falls. I remember my excitement when I first saw them, how the bare viewpoint sloped unprotected toward the yawning, sickening drop and how the thin column of water fell and fell, so slowly and hypnotically that I had clung to a thin, well-polished tree growing close to the edge and wrenched my eyes away. I take E.F. there proudly, as if the awesome magnificence of the spectacle is all my own work. But I might have known what to expect.

"It does look a bit feeble," he says, "after Niagara."

We are going our separate ways. E.F. is no longer the groomed individual he was when he first arrived. His face is burned unevenly by the sun, a red-nosed, peeling burn, so different from his customary even tan. His hair is awry and his beard ragged; altogether, he looks a lot more human. But in two days' time, he will be in Köln, and he will no doubt soon rectify the situation.

I cut across the plateau and pick up the surveyor's trail that will take me back down to Lonesome Lake. The coveted binoculars are in my pocket, for my friend suddenly and generously gave them to me when we parted. I pause for a nibble at the little, icy creek, then pound down the steep, knee-wrenching trail. The distant roar of the Atnarko comes up from the bottom of the valley to meet me. As the trees grow taller and the wind's voice deepens, I think of the time that I have spent in E.F.'s company. I have a strong suspicion that, for all his complaining, he has really enjoyed himself. I am willing to bet that the experiences of the past few days will stay with him for a long time. I can imagine him describing the hardships of the trail to his city friends and saying, "Now I know I can do anything." He will remember his achievements but not his discomforts, and that is how it should be.

Chapter 8
Building the Walls

Before I came here from Salmon Arm, I spent some time watching a professional log builder and his employees at work. They were constructing several houses at a time. After they were completed, the houses would be allowed to settle for a year, then they would be dismantled and trucked to the clients' sites. In the hands of experts such as these, notching looks easy. The saws are handled with the precision of a dentist's drill, and they caress the curved surface of the cut as if stroking the shell of an egg. When the log is finished and rolled into place, the joints are flawless, smooth and Inca-tight.

The professional builders were not very keen for me to practise on their logs, so all I could do was watch closely and, once I returned to my own building site, try to remember the procedure. First, I have to put the logs into position so that the notches can be measured. Following the Turners' advice, I place poles so that they angle between the ground and one end of each of the outside foundation logs: held in position with a nail, they form skids up which I can roll the next layer of logs. These will be the floor joists. There will be nine of them, and as they straddle all four foundation logs, each one will require 4 notches, that is 36 notches in all.

With two people and a couple of peaveys, raising the joists such a short distance does not pose a problem; and once they are on the foundation logs, they can be manoeuvred with ease and I can work alone.

The outside floor joist will also be the bottom wall log at the east end of the house, the one farthest from the river. It will form the shorter side of the L. I position the log and, with a pencil, draw a rough notch around each proposed joint. I flip the log onto its back, wedge it with rocks and start the smaller of my two saws. I make vertical cuts about an inch apart to the edges of the pencil mark and knock out the unwanted wood with a three-pound hammer. The inside of the notch is left with little steps from which the slices of wood have been split. So far, so good.

Now comes the eggshell trick. I fire up the saw again, expecting the bar to glide gently around the curve, but the saw has other ideas. It is designed to cut straight, and in an instant, the teeth are slicing well past my pencil marks. I try using just the tip of the bar, but the saw kicks in an alarming manner and my forearms are soon numb from the vibrations.

Still, these are only the rough notches. When they are done, I flip the log into position again so that more accurate ones can be drawn. This is done with a set of scribes, a tool like a compass, with a point on one end and a pencil on the other. By simultaneously running the point over the foundation log and pressing the pencil against the cross log, I reproduce exactly the contours of the joint.

Making the saw follow the curve is, however, a different kettle of fish. I hack the notches out somehow, but the edges are spiky with slivers and the fit is anything but perfect. It is a good thing these first cuts will all be hidden beneath the floorboards.

After 36 attempts, I have improved a little, but now I must tackle the first north-wall log, which is 26 feet long. It requires not only the nine notches to fit over the ends of all the floor joists but also a lateral groove to marry it snugly to the foundation log below it. This is a chain-saw adaptation of the Scandinavian method used in the axe-hewn log buildings that were prevalent at one time down the valley.

Making the lateral groove is not easy. First, the log must be rough-notched. Then the scribes must be set wide enough to accommodate all the notches as well as to copy the irregularities of the bottom log onto the underside of the upper one. I now discover that a chain saw, especially one with standard teeth, does not take kindly to ripping wood. Not only is it hard on the machine, using an enormous amount of gas, but it is back-breaking for the operator. If I ever do this again, I will fit a larger saw with a ripping chain specifically to use for the lateral grooves. But now that I have started on the building, I cannot bear the thought of wasting the time to go out to buy one.

When I clunk the notched log back into position, it fits so badly that I have to rescribe it and cut it all over again. It takes me two days to reach a degree of finish I feel I can put up with. But once again, I have to heave the log onto its back so that I can stuff strips of fibreglass batts into the grooves and notches. Finally, the log is flipped over again and chivvied into position with the peavey. There, I hope, it will stay.

The walls have grown higher; the skids, longer and steeper. I can now use the saw with some accuracy, but my scribing is not always very good, especially where I have had to use the tops of tree trunks as building logs. These are full of knots, and even though I have tried to smooth them, they are still bumpy.

Being L-shaped, the house has six walls. If things are going well, I can manage three logs, or half a round, in a day. Every evening, the Turners come over and help me raise the next day's quota. The house is growing rapidly, and I am elated with my progress.

As the walls become too high for the skids, we must use gin poles to raise the logs. These are vertical posts set inside the corners of the building, roped to the foundation and guyed to the opposite walls. From the gin poles, we hang blocks and tackle to lift the heaviest logs.

Now, however, I am running into other problems. I can no longer reach the tops of the walls from the ground; I have to learn to balance on the corners of the logs to cut the notches and shuffle backward along the top of the wall while making the lateral groove. The saw's ragged teeth seem perilously close to my feet, and as the distance to the ground increases alarmingly with every round of logs, I must shut out of my mind the thought of a fall.

Things are beginning to go wrong with the little saw I have been using for the log work. Under Jack's guidance, I take the carburetor apart, revealing microscopic pieces of machinery of whose existence and function I had not the slightest idea. Bolts have sheared or simply shaken out of the casing, and I try to hold the saw together by bandaging it with fencing wire. One day, it refuses to start at all, and I resort to using the bigger saw. The bar is longer, which makes it much more difficult and dangerous to handle, and its kick is tremendous. It bucks me off the wall twice. Both times I land unhurt, but once I feel the wind of whirring teeth on my bare arm. It gives me such a fright that I have to steel myself to look at my arm to make sure it is still there.

Rain also hampers me. Not only does it become suicidal to handle the logs, but even if I can complete the lateral groove (which I now find easier to finish with a chisel), I cannot work with the insulation, because once it is wet, it is useless. Sometimes I must wait until the Turners have time to haul more logs. The wet summer has rendered the haymaking frustrating, and some of the work must be done over and over again. In the meantime, the logs still lying within the gloom of the forest have grown black with mould, always a problem with summer-fallen trees, as the mould thrives on sap. This might have been avoided had I been able to drag the

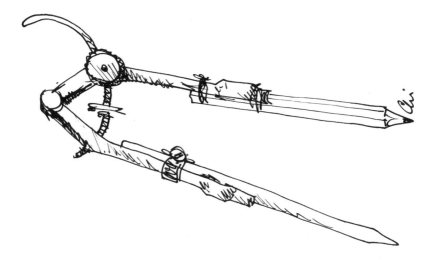

logs into the open and raise them off the ground as soon as they were peeled. But without the horses, I couldn't manage it.

Finally, the big saw, too, gives up the ghost. The bar-tightening nut has sheared; I don't have a spare, and I can't fix it with fencing wire. So I fill my pack with greasy machinery and go down the valley for repairs.

It is now the beginning of September, and this weekend is the Bella Coola Valley Fall Fair. To an outsider, it might seem a drab spectacle: the main building is an asbestos-roofed arch, unlined and unadorned; inside, the lighting is poor, the display space inadequate and the standard of entries not always very good. But whereas many of the larger centres might put on shows visually more attractive, I bet they are not half as much fun.

In such community events, everyone participates – no one is a stranger. On the Thursday before the fair weekend, entries are brought in. People arrive with fat turnips, impossible cabbages, baking, needlework and pickles. The heavy scent of flowers fills the building, and children scamper between the tables clutching various works of art. Friday is judging day, and on Saturday, the valley folk rush in to see who received the red cards and who the coveted first-place blue. That the flowers have started to wilt and the baking looks a little dry does not really matter. There are the parade, the fancy dress, the speeches, the tractor-drawn train rides and the delicious pies that were made by the women who operate the Co-op coffee bar during the rest of the year. In the afternoon, logging sports test the skills of axemen and chain sawyers. Our women's tug-of-war team cannot compete with the superior weight of the Credit Union team, and I am ashamed to say, in the women's nail-driving contest, I do not even place.

The summer is suddenly over. Since my return home two days ago, the wind has changed, the temperature has crashed, and a wild storm has driven snow well down the sides of the valley. When the clouds dissolve, the mountain gradually emerges, and it gleams in dazzling winter splendour, etched with porcelain-blue shadows. Three days of clear skies have produced hard night frosts and brought out a last flush of blackflies that tramp heavy-footed across my face and arms in a last, desperate attempt to feed and reproduce before winter. When I was first exposed to these little monsters, they left behind huge, itching lumps that nearly drove me to distraction and took days to subside. My face was covered with pestilent swellings: I looked as though I suffered from some exotic plague. The bites no longer affect me, but I cannot get used to the crawling.

The garden seems a blackened ruin. But the potatoes are safe underground; we dig them, then haul the pea vines into the barn and hang them from racks in the rafters to dry. Despite their dubious appearance, they will make acceptable feed for the cows. Our own diet is suddenly full of apples as the windfalls in the Turners' orchard thump relentlessly to the ground. The forest has become a shimmer of colour. The pastel browns and burgundies of the sarsaparilla are scattered with the glowing embers of bunchberries and the gold of discarded birch leaves. Autumn is upon us.

Chapter 9

The Salmon Run

The Atnarko River is an exciting place in the fall, for along its length spawn four of the five species of Pacific salmon. Each breed has its own time and territory, and it is sockeyes that concentrate in the stretch of water that runs through the homestead. Their struggle to swim upriver after four or five years at sea, their fight for the very stones over which they were hatched and their lingering and dramatic deaths are endlessly intriguing to me.

When the fish first come into the river in mid-July, they are barely noticeable, for their bodies are as silvery as a water ripple, and they lie in the pools by day, travelling on at night. But sometimes as I swam beside the cottonwood logs at Horseshoe Bend, a large, broad-finned shadow loomed momentarily in an eddy; if the light was right, I could distinguish squadrons of dark shapes in the bottoms of the deepest pools.

The journey upriver takes two to three months. During that time, the fish undergo a startling metamorphosis. Their streamlined silver bodies become humped and ruby-red, and their bottle-green heads elongate into vicious hooked beaks rimmed with splayed, bony teeth. The fish need no food once they leave the salt water, and the teeth develop solely as weapons to slash the flesh of their rivals into tattered ribbons.

At the beginning of September, the salmon suddenly abandon the shelter of the pools and begin to claim territories above the gravel bars. Against the golden, sun-rippled pebbles and glacier-green pools, their crimson bodies glow like stained glass shot through with light. Within a week, they are thick across the river, each pair of fish a foot or two apart. The current is swift over the shallows, and the fish have to swim vigorously to maintain their places.

They are possessed by an excessive energy that drives them to leap far clear of the water or wriggle frantically up places with so little depth that their bodies are half-exposed. These blind urges seem pointless, for they allow themselves to drift back into their old territories again, often minus a shred of flesh if they have travelled too close to a rival. The continuous slap and splash of their exertions can be heard day and night above the gravelly chatter of the river.

It is most fascinating to watch them from the trail above the pool at the foot of the Stillwater. The humpbacks gather there, as well as a few sockeyes. They can be seen diving deep, then swimming violently to the surface in water so clear that it is impossible to discern the fine line between it and the air until the fish erupt in a glittering explosion of spray. These writhing, smaller fish are a direct contrast to the much larger spring salmon which also share the pool and which will travel far upriver to spawn above the homestead. They lie close to the bank, almost motionless, like vast, pink torpedoes.

The sockeye run peaks at the end of September. The spawning takes place at night; I have never seen it, but sometimes, during daylight, one of the partners will flip onto its side and stir up a puff of sand with a graceful undulation of its tail. It must require considerable strength to move the strawberry-sized stones that cover most of the riverbed. The coral-pink eggs would be whisked away by the river if they were not buried at once. A few of the millions of eggs escape into the backwaters, and these are eagerly sought by trout, mergansers and other predators.

After spawning, the fish begin to die. When they first spread across the gravel bars, some already bear a thick, white streak along their backs – a parasitic fungus that will eventually cover them completely. From their backs, it spreads in rosettes and blotches. Their body colours fade, and their fins and tails become tattered and threadbare. But still they fight and sway and slither until, one by one, they succumb, drifting downstream on their sides, ringed eyes staring, struggling feebly. No doubt their brains have disintegrated with their bodies, but it is impossible to be unmoved as the still splendid fish glint and tumble in the whirlpools and wash up onto the gravel bars. The bodies rot, and the ravens peck out the eyes.

At the beginning of October, the river begins to smell. By Thanksgiving, I think it expedient to haul drinking water from a fresh creek across the river, but before long, the fall rains sweeten the air. Downstream, between the Stillwater and Stuie, where the river splits and braids into many channels, the humpback spawn in huge numbers and the smell of the dead becomes overpowering, lingering for weeks.

For those with palates less finicky than ours, the life-and-death throes of the salmon provide an orgy of food. Predatory fish such as sculpins seek the unburied eggs; kingfishers, great grey herons and mergansers eat the smaller fish; otters are admirably equipped to catch the larger ones; and ravens, crows, gulls and bald eagles congregate for anything that is offered.

Eagles are lazy creatures and great thieves. Sometimes they stoop for their own meal, but usually they prefer to harass others. Once I heard the most spine-chilling, croaking shriek: an eagle had attacked a heron, no doubt for the fish it carried, and the two vastly different birds gyrated through a strange and awkward ballet before flying apart. They were too far away for me to see what happened to the prey, but judging by their subsequent flight patterns, neither ended up with the fish. On another occasion, an eagle stood a few paces away from three otters on a bank. The otters were unafraid of the eagle and totally ignored her. The eagle, however, was very interested in the otters' meal. She looked hard at the animals, shuffled sideways for a couple of steps, then took to the air. Two heavy wing beats brought her to the otters, who, without haste, slid effortlessly into the water with their fish, popping out again the minute the bird had passed. The frustrated eagle turned slowly and swooped once more, but the otters took no notice of her and she beat away in disgust.

The eagles' favourite targets are the ospreys. These large, white-fronted hawks are briefly common in the fall, and I often hear them plop into the water in pursuit of a meal. Usually, they fly up again empty-footed, but one time, a bird splashed into the river in front of the house and seemed unable to rise. Half smothered, it appeared to be drowning in the swift current, but flapping its wings, it reached a back eddy and was able to scramble onto a gravel bar. In its feet was a large trout. The osprey shook the water from its feathers and stood a moment to rest. As it took off, the fish gave a violent wriggle and the bird had to readjust its grip. No doubt, the osprey was hoping to reach its favourite perch on top of a big fir, but the weight of the fish was dragging it down, and it could gain height only with difficulty. Down swooped the eagle. There was a moment of confusion, a splash, and the lightened osprey soared away. It had lost the fish, but so had the eagle. In fact, I never saw a robbery that was successful.

There is one important guest at this annual banquet who cannot be treated with such dispassionate interest: the grizzly. Although I have seen one only briefly, I cannot help being aware of its reputation. I have a suspicion that the danger is grossly exaggerated, for most wild animals prefer to keep well away from the human species and its chattels. An accident becomes newsworthy only if it is rare, and grizzly attacks are so unusual that they easily make headlines. Very few people will ever have the privilege of seeing a grizzly, let alone have an alarming encounter with one. Nonetheless, the animal has great strength, formidable claws and teeth and an uncertain temper, and it is, without a doubt, potentially dangerous. So when huge, spiked footprints appear in the soft mud banks by the edge of the river, I am glad to take the Turners' advice and move from my camp into Trudy's original claim cabin. It is 8 by 14 feet, and Trudy built it unaided in eight days, using only an axe. It now functions only as a storage shed, and although the roof has been maintained, it no longer has a door or windows. However, as it is some distance from the water and not on a game trail, it is a lot safer than my tent. Grizzlies have never attempted to enter any buildings here.

It is cold in the evenings now. The little, rusty camp stove is so decrepit that it cannot be risked inside the cabin, so I have erected it on a bed of gravel under the porch. It gives little warmth, particularly when the wind blows, and I huddle round it only long enough to cook and eat my supper before crawling into my sleeping bag on the split-cedar floor.

The mornings are sharp with frost, and breakfast over, I am glad to start work and warm my numb feet; my boots are disintegrating, and the ice on the grass melts through the split seams. The river is bluish in the early light, and through the miasma of mist, the swaying salmon are dull and indistinct. I have the silly thought that they feel cold, for it makes me shiver to look at them.

The sun rises late, shining first on the new snow on the mountain, then creeping slowly down the western side of the valley before flooding the fields and my homesite with instant warmth. The diamond fires of frost glitter briefly and spectacularly; as the sun touches them, golden birch leaves drop like coins in the windless air.

On with the ear protectors and down with the head: for the rest of the day, I am oblivious to everything, barring the maniacal scream of the saw and the sluggish crawl of the blackflies as they tramp their rounds again.

Chapter 10
The Holiday

Jack Turner spent part of his youth on Saltspring Island, off the coast of British Columbia. He wants to go back there and take Trudy with him; it will be his first visit in 40 years. It is one thing to leave the homestead to fend for itself for a couple of days, as the Turners have often done on mail trips or on brief excursions into the mountains, but it is quite another to abandon it for two weeks. Until I came along, there was no one available to look after the animals for so long. I will not be able to work on the house while they are away, as I cannot roll the logs up unaided, so it will be a holiday for me too.

As the plane roars away, a feeling of exultation overwhelms me. The Turners are the best of neighbours, never intruding and always ready to help, but now, for a while, I can be truly alone. It is the greatest freedom on this Earth.

I bask in the sunshine and try to decide what to do first. Read? Go for a walk? Dig out my sadly neglected art supplies and paint? Have a bath? Or merely fritter away the time in idleness?

First, a bath seems in order. The river is too chilly for me now, so I heat water in the washtub over the stove and place it in a sunny patch on the grass. For some time, my hair has been irritating me by flopping into my eyes and dragging on my collar. I know it needs cutting, but when I look

in a mirror that I have borrowed from the Turners, I get quite a shock. How wild and ragged I have grown! My hair sticks out and is dull and stiff with sawdust. My clothes, bearing the marks of a summer's hard usage, are ripped and blotched with dirt-blackened resin. My mother would disown me. I prop the mirror against the washtub on the grass and begin to cut. The cows are grazing nearby: black-and-white Valerian and red-and-white Clarian (spelled with an "a," as her name is a mixture of letters from her parents' names) with their two half-grown calves. They are always eager for new entertainment and come and stand in a solemn circle, chewing their cud and watching my every move.

When the mountain shadow is halfway up the valley wall, it is time to prepare the cow for milking. Clarian is dry, but Valerian is fresh. I have milked cows in commercial dairy herds all over the world and have known thousands of animals, each of them different. City people are surprised at this: either they forget that each dog or cat they have encountered has a different personality, or they assume that cows have a vastly reduced intelligence. Any creatures herded together in large numbers lose their character, including humans. To me, city people are frighteningly alike, aspiring to be carbon copies of each other. Their programmed world gives them no chance to grow as individuals; not only are they unbelievably ignorant about what goes on beyond the limits of their lives, but they also surmise that anything outside their range of experience is inferior and not worth knowing.

But back to cows. Each herd will have as full a spectrum of personalities as any group of people. There are fat ones, thin ones, greedy ones, gentle ones, crabby ones, timid ones and bossy ones. Most of them adapt readily to the environment into which they are introduced when they first calve, but they are creatures of habit. As long as their whims are catered to, things go smoothly; give them something new, however, and they can be as stubborn as anything in creation. If they wish to object, their feet, horns and bodily strength can make them formidable adversaries. So to preserve both Valerian's equanimity and my sanity, I must respect her idiosyncrasies and stick to her routine.

First, all the animals are tied up. In winter, they would be in the barn, but now, a tree or fence suffices—providing it is a tree or fence that they are used to. Then they are given a bucket of vegetables, mostly potatoes and kitchen waste. Clarian will not eat apples, but Valerian gobbles them up; Valerian likes her food tipped on the ground and ignores it otherwise, but when Clarian has crunched through the cabbage leaves and potatoes, she likes to play with the bucket, licking it rhythmically round the edge. The infernal clanking is enough to drive anyone crazy.

The calf is allowed to suck before I begin milking. Valerian has large, tough teats like great parsnips. The back ones are the hardest to milk, so I gently hold the front ones while the overgrown offspring butts and slobbers over the back ones. I drag him off and tie him up again long before he is satisfied—he no longer needs the milk, but the cow is used to it and she will not let her milk down otherwise. As my touch is unfamiliar to Valerian, my hands and the way I squeeze will no doubt feel quite different from Trudy's, so I rope the cow's back leg as a precaution. She does not kick, but at first, she fidgets until I realize that she does not like my knee jammed against her belly. I am much taller than Trudy, and the sawed-off log she uses as a milking stool is too high for me. When I find another one that gives more room for my legs, the cow is perfectly happy; her gross stomach gurgles placidly close to my ear, and the tough teats gradually become flaccid and empty. I am out of practice and my hands ache—it will take a couple of days before I no longer feel the strain.

I have to untie the animals in the right order, for Valerian is boss, and if she is let loose first, she will hook the others with her horns. Tied, they will be unable to get away, but if they are free, they can easily avoid her.

The milk must be filtered, then set to cool in a pail in the river. The previous day's milk has to be skimmed and the cream pasteurized, then cooled again in a sterilized bucket. That way, it will keep until Trudy comes home, when she will make butter with it.

The two weeks are almost over, and I have done very little but enjoy my solitude. With my head bent perpetually over the logs and my hearing muffled by the ear protectors all summer, I have been able to observe very little of my surroundings. Now I can indulge myself. Sometimes I go back to the lagoon and hang in the canoe over the reflections of the yellow birch trees, or I hike to Tenas Lake, three miles upriver. This is a small, pretty oval fringed with birches and backed by the seamed and broken summits of Mount Ada. The trail that leads there winds through a swampy cedar forest whose floor is thick with waxy, newly fallen cottonwood leaves. The dwindling sun no longer penetrates the forest, and everything is dark and dank. Huge mushrooms, pale as moons and slick with rain, shine like saucer-sized eyes in the gloom. When the weather socks in and ribbons of cloud stripe the valley walls, I sit by the stove in my sleeping bag and wade luxuriously through the Turners' extensive collection of books.

The rest and relaxation have been marvellous. After my neighbours return, I work feverishly on the remaining logs. One frosty night, while I shovel down my supper by lamplight and a tiny, icy wind tries to find its way down the back of my neck, I hear a faint and melodious clamouring, a soft trumpeting like a traffic jam of motorless toy cars. It is the first of the trumpeter swans arriving from their breeding grounds in Alaska. These huge white birds of the snows are the heralds of winter. As they arrive, I must depart, for there is no shelter for me here now that the weather is deteriorating. I shall go out to Stuie for the winter and leave my L-shaped walls open to the sky and greying in the late fall rains.

Chapter 11
Second Spring

My Stuie neighbours have gone to Ontario for the winter — Katie wants to finish a degree she started 20 years ago — so I am wintering there alone. Rather than use the large, uninsulated house, I put a good stove in one of the rental cabins, which is smaller and therefore much easier to heat. Although Stuie is not much lower than Lonesome Lake, it is closer to the coast and consequently both warmer and wetter: I am very glad of a warm roof over my head, but I am disconcerted by the lack of snow and surfeit of rain. Nevertheless, the winter passes quietly and uneventfully; by spring, I am ready to start work again.

I would love to go back upriver as soon as the snow melts in March, but I would have neither food nor fuel for the saw, so once again, I have to wait until the lake at Nimpo opens at the end of May before I can fly in the necessary supplies.

I hike upriver to the homestead a day or two before the plane is due and backpack my goods from the little claim cabin to my summer enclosure. But I do not want to set up camp before the plane comes, for it is bringing a large, old canvas tent, a gift from a valley woman, now living at Hagensborg, who once pioneered the Stillwater.

It is also bringing a cat and two ladies aged 78 and 82, women I knew years ago in England. I have warned them that conditions in my camp will

be somewhat primitive, but they are keen to come, and being both British (and therefore used to cold and damp) and from a farm, they will probably cope with my inconveniences better than most.

I walk down to the lagoon to meet the plane. It is a hot, humid morning. The ladies bought a gallon of ice cream at the Nimpo Lake store, a present for the Turners, who rarely taste such treats; although we float it in the lagoon while we unload the plane, it is already melting. Most of my freight can stay by the wharf for the time being, but we have to bring home my friends' personal gear, the tent and, of course, the cat, who is travelling, under loud protest, in a box.

Pussy Cat is still a kitten, with fluffy, grey fur and beguiling eyes just changing from blue to green. Soft and innocent she may look, but already, she has a very definite mind of her own. She does not like the box. She screamed in the bus all the way to Nimpo Lake from Bella Coola. She cried in the plane: I hear her as soon as the motor is switched off and the plane drifts to the wharf. She wails loudly and rhythmically while we unload the freight on the wharf, and she screeches every step of the way along the trail, strapped on top of the load on my backpack. She is instantly silent the moment she is let out of the box—it was all she ever wanted. She starts exploring the campsite's clutter with great contentment.

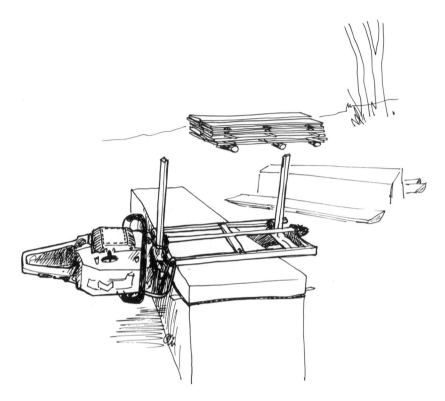

The tent poses an unexpected problem. It is 35 years since it was last used, and although I unrolled it to check it for holes before I flew it in, I did not attempt to erect it. It is a ridge tent, but it must have originally had a freestanding internal frame, for there are no means of hanging it from a traditional external one and nothing to which guy ropes can be attached.

The overly hot morning has given us a thundery afternoon. My guests and our possessions are in imminent danger of getting wet. I hack some cedar poles from the bush, make holes in the ends of the tent to accommodate guys and eventually rig up a structure that works. We throw our belongings into the musty interior and, as the first fat drops of rain fall, fling the blue tarp over everything and tie it down. We make it just before the heavens open.

We have forgotten about the cat.

Although we gave most of the ice cream to the Turners, we kept some in a quart jar to eat for lunch. The empty jar was abandoned on the grass, and earlier in the afternoon, the kitten was found inside, head first and licking greedily, her pretty, fluffy hair all matted with the residue. We hauled her out and promptly forgot her as we struggled to set up camp, but now, as the rain begins to drum on the tarp, a piercing wail rises above the noise. The stove has not been erected, and sections of the chimney lie beside it. The ice-cream-sticky cat has crawled into one of these and is now plastered with soot. Despite her vigorous vocal protests, I take her down to the river in the pouring rain and clean her long fur with a pot scrub.

My guests have a busy schedule and have to leave after a day or two. The plane that fetches them is loaded to capacity with more supplies, and once again, the Turners, Lucky and I pack everything up to the homestead. While I was away during the winter, my enormous brush piles were burned, and the clearing now looks like the aftermath of a nuclear holocaust. Stumps and huge logs, too twisted and knotty for use and too dense to be digested by the flames, lie blackened on the ground, charred monuments to our feeble efforts to destroy them.

The first major job before me is turning into lumber those logs which were too fat for building. Last summer, I bucked them into 13-foot lengths, and now, I have to submit to the excruciating miseries and frustrations of the chain saw as I slice them into boards. For floors, ceilings, window framing and doors, I estimate I will need 400 boards. To make them, I will use an Alaskan Mill, a device that converts my chain saw into a lumber mill. Basically, it is a metal frame consisting of two uprights bolted onto the base and the tip of the bar. These uprights support a horizontal cutting guide that sits on top of the log. The distance between the guide and the bar can be adjusted to produce lumber of varying thickness. Once the guide is fixed, I cut horizontally through the log from butt to tip. But the mill needs a flat surface to sit on, and I cannot lop off the rounded side of the log accurately enough by eye. I need a board to tack onto the tree trunk to guide my first cut, but where will I find it? There is not a piece of sawn lumber on the place. The Turners split all their boards from cedar, axing them smooth when necessary, and they have gradually covered their floors and walls with plywood.

One day, I discover an old, water-worn plank, 10 feet long, floating in the lagoon. This rare and opportune find is no doubt an escapee from the old sawmill, long since derelict, that Trudy's father built on his homestead at the head of the lake. I strap the board vertically onto my pack frame and backpack it home, catching every overhanging branch on the way. I nail it on top of the first log, ready to receive the mill.

I have the idea that for ripping, the teeth on the saw chain have to be modified, but advice from my log-building friends is not consistent; few have had much experience with making lumber with a chain saw. One recommended a commercial ripping chain with alternating fat and thin teeth, all filed at an angle of 45 degrees; another told me to take a crosscut chain and file it to 5 degrees. Will Malloff, the author of my primary reference book, *Chainsaw Lumbermaking*, insists that the only way is to use a chisel-cut chain filed straight across.

I start with the commercial ripping chain on my biggest saw, the one with a 30-inch bar. When the mill is bolted to the chain-saw bar, it is very heavy and difficult to lift onto the guide board. With the motor screaming full blast, the chain begins to bite into the butt end of the log, and, infinitesimally slowly, millimetre by millimetre, it creeps along. On my knees beside it, I am choked with fumes and nearly drowned with fountaining sawdust. Long before the end of the log, the saw runs out of gas. It takes about half an hour to cut that first board and two days to reduce the log to lumber. The thought of the other 394 boards is soul-destroying.

I think one of my troubles is that the saw is not powerful enough, but with money tight, I had to buy one I could use for both falling and milling. The next size up would have been too heavy for me to use in the bush.

Although my incompatibility with machines severely hampers me, I gradually learn how to solve some of the problems of lumber making. The slightest variation in the air/fuel mix or in the angle of the teeth makes a great deal of difference to the performance of the saw. I find that Malloff is right: the saw works best when the teeth are filed straight across. But when the performance is still not up to scratch, I am never sure what the problem is. I might spend hours filing the teeth when it is the rakers that need adjusting, or waste time attempting to clean the carburetor when it is a blocked filter that is at fault. When the bar becomes worn on one side and the saw stalls because it tries to dig itself into the log, it takes me days to work that one out. The machinery breaks with monotonous regularity, and I seem to be spending all my time packing heavy equipment back and forth to the highway.

It is a hot, dry summer, with scorching temperatures that are intensified by the great, unshaded patches of black ashes strewn in the clearing. The dust, the fumes, the gritty sawdust in my eyes and clothes, the flies that crawl over undefended hands and face and, worst of all, the unending scream of the motor, which, despite protectors, leaves my ears buzzing, would be unendurable were I not working for myself. No money in the world would tempt me to go through that for anyone else. One memorable day, I cut 30 boards, but on another of black despair, I manage only 2. Gradually, however, the stacks of lumber pile up on the riverbank, each layer of boards separated by inch-wide laths to allow the boards to dry. The top one is weighted heavily to prevent warping. By the middle of summer, I have enough.

Somehow, I have found time to put in a bit of a garden. The Turners ploughed up land for me next to their own plot within the seven-foot-high deer fence. There is soil on that side of the river, a fine silt which whirls away into dust as soon as it dries but packs so densely when wet that the water cannot drain through it; it quickly becomes sour and starved for oxygen. There is no compost to put on it, for deciduous trees are few and all vegetable leaves and peelings go to feed the cows. There is not enough of the precious barn manure to go around, and artificial fertilizer adds no tilth to the soil.

I do not have a green thumb. No matter how much energy I put into preparing the soil and weeding, my plants look sickly and yield poorly. The Turners' crops next door to mine are twice the size. The growing season is short, with killing frosts as late as mid-June and as early as the beginning of September. Many plants have to be started under glass, and beans, tomatoes, corn and squash have to be covered on every clear night. But with care, providing the hardiest varieties are chosen, quite an array of stuff can be raised: asparagus, potatoes, carrots, parsnips, the cabbage family, onions, beans and peas, even green peppers.

A day in the garden is a relief from the torture of the saw, but my aching muscles would rather I did something other than crawl on hands and knees, pecking with my fingers at embryonic weeds among microscopic carrots. Some of the weeds, such as lamb's quarters and sheep sorrel, are edible, even delicious, and I graze along the rows, grateful for the green nibbles, for they are the only fresh vegetables I will have for some time.

On my first mail run, I have the good fortune to acquire a second canoe. I am overjoyed, for although the Stillwater is the smallest lake on the journey to the highway, the scramble around it is by far the toughest part of the trip. When you can drive all the way to the footbridge, the distance from the Stillwater to the tote road is only three miles. As I have often carried 80-pound loads that far, I assume I will have no trouble portaging the canoe. Fortunately, as it is the middle of summer, the washout has dried up, and early one morning, I drive all the way in from Stuie. I ease the canoe out of the truck and prop it upside down against the cab. The makeshift yoke settles comfortably on my shoulders, and I straighten my legs and set off confidently up the trail. Within yards, my shoulders are in agony. I look frantically for a suitable branch to support the bow and give myself a rest. Through the forested sections of the trail, it is not so bad, for such branches are plentiful, but crossing the rock slides is murder. The trail climbs twice over steep bluffs. Going down them is the worst, for I have to tip the canoe forward to keep the stern clear of the ground behind me yet keep my body back to balance the load; at the same time, I need to look down at the loose stones beneath my feet. The river boils at the foot of the bluff, and the noise, trapped by the hull, booms about my ears. The sky promises rain, the only wet day of summer so far, and the mosquitoes have found that my elongated umbrella is a marvellous place for lunch. As my arms are locked onto the gunwales of the canoe, I can do nothing about them. I have never been so thankful to reach the Stillwater and relieve my back of the load.

I go back to the tote road for my pack and return with another 80-pound load, which includes my sleeping bag, a box of groceries, a typewriter and three gallons of chain oil. When I reach the lake, the rain is quite heavy, and I open the pack to pull out a coat. One of the containers of chain oil has leaked. Chain oil is made especially sticky to combat the centrifugal force of the whirling chain: my coat is a solid lump of treacly, red oil, impossible to clean or wear. Luckily, the sleeping bag and typewriter are well wrapped in garbage bags, but I have to finish the journey unprotected from the rain. I clean all the gear as best I can, but I shall never get the oil out of the pack.

Chapter 12

Raising the Roof

After the stress of lumber making, cutting the roof poles seems easy. The trees that I fall are light and slim and far less terrifying than the giants I tackled last summer. As July is well advanced, the bark has loosened and they peel easily. The Turners and their horses take time out from haying to come over and haul the poles to the site.

Before starting the roof, there is one small job that has to be done—cutting a door hole. It is no longer practical to scramble over the corners of the walls as we have been doing. Experienced log builders cut the door and window holes as they erect the walls, but last summer, all I could think about were the logs; besides, I did not yet have all the window frames. These have since been gleaned in an assortment of sizes from dumps and abandoned houses; they were flown in on the same plane that had fetched my English ladies. Logic tells me that the solid, fortlike construction, which has been standing for several months now, will remain as firm as ever when I cut a hole in it, but I have the awful feeling, as the saw is poised for its long, vertical slice through the logs, that the whole structure will fall apart. It doesn't, of course. In fact, even after I have courageously cut through the logs to create the doorway, the timbers remain so tightly wedged together that it is only by using a lot of leverage with a wrecking bar and pounding with a sledgehammer that I am able to dislodge them.

I have not the slightest idea how I am going to raise the rafters and heavy purlins – the long, horizontal stringers that support the roofing; but as the Turners' barn is much higher, I know there has to be a simple method. Sure enough, Trudy, who began her apprenticeship with her father at an early age, has a solution to every problem. With a combination of skids, gin poles, peaveys and pulleys, anything can be accomplished.

In my ignorance, I assume that the roof will be finished in a couple of weeks, but it drags on for months. First, I find it alarming to be perched so high off the ground, and until a fair amount of the framework has been completed, I feel so insecure that I move only one limb at a time, like a chameleon. Second, it takes three times as long to do anything at the top of two sets of ladders. Tools are dropped or left on the ground, and precious time must be spent building scaffolding and altering it as requirements change. Third, round, not-quite-straight logs take a lot of fitting onto a not-quite-square building. And fourth, I need help more frequently. The Turners always come when they can, but they are busy with their own work – the garden and the hay – and are not always available.

Gradually, the roof takes shape. The ridgepole runs directly above the second foundation log, creating a saltbox roof with a short, steeply pitched north slope and a long, gently sloping south face which extends the full width of the house at the back but which is cut short at the front by the L. Here, I build a kneewall to fill the gap between the log walls and the roofline. From the ridgepole, I run rafters to the eaves – the extra-long timbers that cover the back south slope are particularly heavy and awkward to handle. Next come the purlins. When the porch, with its overhanging roof, is defined, the whole character of the building changes. About halfway along the north side of the roof, I position the chimney, fitting it carefully through the grid of the roof structure so that the insulated sections of stovepipe are not touching any of the timbers. Now I know exactly where to build the rock-and-concrete platform on the floor for the stove.

I like rafters to be visible from the inside of a house, so I nail the sloping ceiling on top of them, fitting the boards between the purlins. Now I discover just how uneven my hand-sawed lumber is: some boards are humpbacked and others undulate. Their edges are so irregular that all of them have to be planed to fit. But piece by piece, the sky is shut out, and the interior of the building becomes dark and gloomy. With as much trepidation as I had while cutting the doorway, I slice out two window holes to let in some light.

The salmon have started to spread across the gravel bars by the time we are ready for the roofing. As with every aspect of the house, the materials for the roof are dictated by cost and availability. Although there are plenty of cedars in the park, they cannot be touched, and there are not enough left on the property for me to emulate the Turners and make shakes. Metal

roofing is beyond my pocket — all I can afford are thick rolls of tarred paper with a brown, pebbly finish. We put them on in vertical strips, preparing the narrow sections of the roof one at a time, for if the insulation gets wet, it will be ineffective. A layer of plastic goes on top of the ceiling boards, followed by batts of fibreglass; next comes another layer of boards (all tediously planed and fitted on the ground beforehand), and these are held away from the insulation by the purlins, creating a gap for ventilation. Then, a covering of building paper is laid on before the rolled roofing can finally be placed. It is heavy and stiff and easily cracks if it is cold: it can be handled only during the warm part of the day, and the sunshine hours are already short at this time of year. I fasten the rolled roofing with flat-headed nails pounded two or three inches apart along its edges. The south side of the roof has a shallow enough slope to walk on; but to nail the north side, I hang from a rope that I tied round my waist and passed over the ridge to Trudy, who belayed it around the exposed end of a rafter. The rope bites into my lower ribs, and I feel like a sack of potatoes.

It takes several days to reach the halfway point and pass the chimney. That evening, Jack informs me he's heard cubs squalling and seen bear tracks beside the river. It is time to move from my camp.

I could go back to Trudy's claim cabin, but it is such an effort to haul stuff over there. It seems easier to move into the unfinished house, despite the fact that there is no floor, the wind whistles through a 12-inch gap under the walls, the two window holes gape emptily and there is no door to hang in the doorway. This is not the triumphant entry into the complete, clean house that I have held in my mind for so long. I place a few boards on the floor joists in a back corner, and using a wheelbarrow, I relocate my camp, including the protesting cat. It is pouring with rain, and I sit on the boards in a corner of the dry half of the building, watching the water cascade through the uncovered part of the roof.

That evening, as the storm clears, the twilight gathers and the smell of home-canned beef stew (courtesy of the Turners) drifts through the gaps in the walls, a large grizzly ambles into the clearing, coming toward the house on a route his ancestors have no doubt used for centuries. I have always believed that the grizzly myth is greatly exaggerated. However, mentally sneering at other people's horror stories when there is no danger is one thing; when I am confronted with tooth and claw and flesh and blood, I am instantly terrified. My gaping, unprotected window holes suddenly seem far too big. The meaty smell of my supper will surely bring him running. What shall I do?

The dog barks. The bear stops, and a puzzled look comes over his face. "That's funny," he seems to be thinking as he stares toward the house. "Surely that wasn't here last year." Then he leisurely turns and walks, without haste, back into the forest.

The weather improves, and the roof is finished at last. The spawning is at its peak. The salmon in the river slither and sway and fight and die; the birch leaves turn golden and begin to drift toward the ground. During last year's spawning season, I saw no bears at all, but at the time, I did not realize how unusual that was. Now, I see grizzlies often as they move quietly through the forest on a game trail behind the house; they are sometimes curious but always peaceful. One sow with two cubs has become quite a fixture. She appears on the tiny island in front of my house, feeding on the white berries of the red willow. For half an hour, she pulls down the bushes and wades in the shallows, her roly-poly youngsters in tow. One cub has a dramatic white "V" on his chest, so the family is easily distinguished. I often watch them from my doorstep in the dusk.

One afternoon, I am sitting on the end of a foundation log that will eventually support my porch. It is hot, and having just eaten lunch, I am half asleep. The cat is dozing on my lap. Suddenly, she growls. I jump awake. Standing in the river is a man. He is wearing chest waders, and he carries a rifle. Unexpected visitors are pretty rare in this part of the country—we might see one or two a year; in any case, they usually come in on the trail. This man is only a few yards away from me, waist-deep in water, staring at me. The chatter of the water has disguised any sound of his approach. He sees that I have noticed him, and he waves, wading slowly toward me.

He has a companion. The two of them reach the ladder propped up against my bank and rise out of the river like misplaced Tritons. I almost expect their green, shining rubber bodies to end in scaly tails.

The men are federal Fisheries officers, and every year, they walk the river to count the spawning salmon. They flew to Tenas Lake first thing this morning, and they will be picked up this evening at the lagoon. They sit on my porch and consume mugs of tea before climbing back down into the water and wading away. Instantly, the view is uninterrupted wilderness, just the singing sparkle of the river and the heavy, golden trees; I have to look twice at the tea mugs to make sure that my visitors were real.

The yellowing leaves and the smell of dying fish mean that very little good weather is left. I must work quickly to finish my shelter. I cut the remaining window holes and fit in my assortment of salvaged frames. I build a heavy door and hang it. I paint the ceiling white and try, with only partial success, to scrub the mould off the wall logs. Finally, I squeeze layers of Styrofoam insulation between the joists and start to lay the floor. My saw gives out again, and I have to solicit Jack's help to trim the final boards. Then they are all down, and suddenly, I have a house. For 18 months, this has been an idea, a dream of the future, and its completion, worked toward for so long, has crept upon me unawares. I sit in the middle of the clean, new, empty floor and marvel at it all. There are many rather drastic mistakes. The sleeping loft that covers half of the interior space is hung too low—I have to duck to walk beneath the joists. One end of the main floor is eight inches higher than the other: it is such a slope that I have had to fit the windows slightly askew to make them look right. My carpentry work around them is pretty crude, partly due to the hogbacks in the boards and partly because of my lack of patience. At the time, speed seemed more important than looks. But it is a house: not just a bush cabin, but a 900-square-foot, L-shaped house. I can close the door and shut out the wind and the rain and the sound of the river; I can enjoy the warmth of the stove and cook and eat my meals in comfort.

And I have built it with my own hands.

Chapter 13
Grizzlies!

It is now the end of October. Very early one morning, I load the ailing saw into my pack and head for the highway. I can see quite well in the clearing, but the darkness is impenetrable in the forest beyond the boundary fence. However, I know the way and am confident I will be able to feel the trail with my feet, something I do quite often. I walk into the blackness. Yards in front of me, a large animal explodes into action and crashes noisily through the bush. "My God! A bear!" I scoot back into the clearing and wait by the barn, heart pounding, until there is enough light to see properly. A bear it was, sure enough, for next to the trail is an anthill, dug up and ripped apart. It can only be a grizzly at this time of year: grizzlies kill and eat black bears, so the two species rarely mix. Fortunately, this grizzly was as frightened as I. It was foolish of me to travel in the dark during the spawning season.

The lagoon is still and grey, and tendrils of mist unfurl from the water like weeds. One of the great advantages of canoeing is its noiselessness. As I slide around a clump of willows, a flock of geese erupts from the water with clamouring cries and beating wings. Behind them, through the shifting mist, stands a huge bull moose. I rest my paddle, and we watch each other. His body is blocky with autumn muscle, and a great rack of antlers spreads over his head like a coffee table. Moose and deer have no

fear of boats and do not seem to associate them with humans; even when I move quite freely or speak to the dog, the bull merely lowers his head and continues his breakfast. I resume my journey, for I don't want to be caught in the dark again at the other end of the day.

A raft of cloud begins to thicken and lower, lopping off the highest points along the walls of the valley. The lake is still motionless, and fish nose pewter rings into the dark, grey-green reflections. Round the last point, cat's-paws ruffle the surface, and I suddenly hit a chilly head wind.

The stretch between the lakes is shrouded in gloom. I keep a very sharp eye out, because here, the river's multiple shallow, gravelly channels are a prime humpback-spawning area and the place is thick with bears. Just before the Stillwater, the forest ends, and the trail, half washed away, is sandwiched between a rock slide and the river. At the top of a rise, blocking the trail only 30 paces away (I measure them later), appears my second grizzly of the day. It is a big, black boar. The wind, quite strong now, is blowing directly toward me. Usually, the dog at my heels warns me if a bear is close, but this one is several feet higher than we are and its scent must be passing over our heads, for the dog is quite unaware of it. The bear and I stare at each other. The frozen moment stretches uncomfortably, and I think it expedient to look for a tree. There aren't many on the rock slide.

Most of the nearest conifers have no branches for at least 50 feet, but three paces behind me, hanging over the river, is a scrubby willow. I turn and stride to it, loosening my pack. I glance at the bear. He is running toward me. Up the tree I go. The dog barks: she has sensed him at last. Another frantic look: the grizzly is galloping flat out—in the opposite direction. I am now sure that he came toward me purely out of curiosity and that when he smelled me, he could not get away fast enough. But I am unable to discuss the matter with him, and it is quite a while before my heartbeat returns to normal.

There are all sorts of theories about the dos and don'ts of bear country. Most accidents happen because the bear feels itself or its cubs are threatened; if surprise close encounters could be avoided, the risk of accident would be greatly reduced. Unfortunately, in this dark and tangled forest, it is very difficult to see the animals in time, and the constant noise of rushing water drowns out sounds that might warn either party. Many people advocate carrying a bell, reasoning that at least the bear will be forewarned, but I have yelled at bears at the top of my voice, and they have not taken the slightest bit of notice. When their heads are buried in a roaring river, far more than a gentle little tinkle is required to alert them. Besides, a bell's clanking and banging irritates me and impairs my own hearing, which I find more useful than sight in such a close environment. Smell seems to be the only thing bears really respond to.

Most bush travellers carry a rifle during spawning season, but I have never fired one and am more frightened of its misuse than I am of the grizzlies. A dog, unless it is strictly under control, can be a disaster, for if it roams loose and discovers a bear, it may run back to its owner for protection, bringing its new acquaintance with it. My dog rarely barks, and she has been trained to stay by my feet on the trail. Her nose is the best bear detector ever invented; as she is terrified of them, I can usually tell by her attitude when they are close. Her ears and tail clamp down as far as they can go, and if the bear is behind us, she walks with her head twisted over her shoulder and bumps into my legs.

However, she is obviously not infallible, and I am still trembling when I reach my canoe at the Stillwater. Despite the head wind, which is pretty strong now, I am more than glad to be away from the shore. At the foot of the lake, I start walking again, and it is not long before I see a dark figure shambling bearlike through a screen of trees. Oh no, not again! But it is only Dennis from Stuie, plodding up the trail after driving up the tote road to meet me.

I am out for a week, and during that time, the weather changes drastically. The temperature crashes to minus 4 degrees F, and its subsequent rise generates a foot of snow. So the journey home is a very different one from my hike down the valley.

It is impossible to drive the tote road, because the walls of brush have been beaten down into a meshed network of branches; it is difficult enough to find a way through on foot, let alone with a vehicle. At times, the snow drags heavily at my feet, but the grizzlies have broken trail for most of the way; the length of their stride is perfect for me, and I walk quite comfortably, like Wenceslas' page, in their footprints.

There is enough current in the old river channel of the Stillwater to keep a sinuous passage open through the lake. It is strange to paddle between wide, white sheets of snow. I have started late, and the short winter day is ending. As I do not want to tackle bears in the dark, I camp under the roofed enclosure that the Turners built to house their boat at the head of the Stillwater and start up between the lakes the next morning.

There are dozens upon dozens of bear tracks of all sizes going in all directions. Many are freckled with the red duff of rotten fir, as the bears like to dig into the remains of disintegrating logs to make their beds. Although I do not see any bears this time, it is astounding to realize how many of these awesome animals make this small area their year-round home.

Hunlen Creek is an unbelievable sight. When the temperature dropped, slush ice, which stayed liquid coming down the falls, congealed upon hitting the boulder fan and flowed sluggishly like white concrete until it froze, gradually spreading over the whole area. The gullies, dry in April and torrential in June, are now completely obscured under a level white mantle. Occasionally, flowing water can be heard gurgling faintly far below. Right at the edge of the lake, buried under several feet of ice, is my canoe. Only one green tip is showing.

Fortunately, the temperature has now warmed to around freezing, and the ice is soft enough to hack away with an axe. The inside of the boat is jammed solid, and the life jacket and paddles must all be chipped free.

The sun has broken through the clouds by the time I glide into the lake, and it has become a glorious afternoon. The bluffs are yellow in the mellow light, and the snow on their ledges is dazzling against a deep blue sky. A bright network of ripple reflections wavers over the rocks along the shore; the air is sharp and sweet and very clear. Near the head of the lake, across the narrowest part, is a barrier of ice. Although it is too thin to walk on, the ice is enough to block the canoe, and I have to pull the boat onto a little point of land and leave it there for the winter.

A couple of hours later, I crunch over the fields of the homestead. The deer fence wriggles like a black worm across the clearing. The sun has gone; the sky is apple-green. It is already freezing hard, so it is going to be very cold tonight. My clearing looks peaceful in the evening light, for the scars of destruction have been hidden under the snow. The house with its yellow logs and smoothly blanketed roof is cozy and welcoming. Pussy Cat, as always, is pleased to see me; her fur is fluffed and crackly with cold.

I dump my pack in the middle of the empty floor and put a match to the stove. I fetch a pail of water from the river, feed the animals, light the lamp and shut the door.

I am home.

Chapter 14

Preparing for Winter

I cannot make seats, shelves or a proper counter, as I have no lumber or proper nails left. Before I can attempt to cut more boards, I will need to buy a new bar for the saw. I have run out of money, so the boards and the nails will have to wait. I can work only with the materials I have at hand. I rig up temporary furniture out of stove lengths and poles lashed together with baling twine. My possessions line the bottoms of the walls in cardboard boxes.

There is a lot of work still to be done outside. The rocky ground will soon freeze, and a proper hole for an outhouse is imperative. I choose a site partially screened by trees, well back from the river and northeast from the house – the wind is least likely to blow from that direction. I was expecting a formidable task in digging the hole, but I encounter surprisingly few roots; none of the rocks is bigger than my head, and I can handle them easily. Around the hole, I build a rickety structure of wood to keep out the worst of the weather, roofing it with the remains of the tarred, pebbled paper.

A chicken house is the next priority. My hens, which were backpacked from the highway as pullets in the spring, have so far been sheltering in the Turners' barn, but that space is now needed by the larger animals. A chicken house in this country must be grizzly-proof. Trudy brings Lucky over the river, and we haul short logs about a foot thick for the walls. The bark is left on, and there is no fancy notching; the ends of the logs are simply squared off and nailed together, then rags, paper feed bags and scraps of fibreglass are pushed into the gaps between the logs for chinking. I nail thin poles both inside and out over the chinking to try to deter the hens and squirrels from pulling it out. I have no roofing left, so I lay several layers of plastic, salvaged from the bags that held fibreglass batts, over a frame of scrap boards and top the lot with the edged, rough-barked slabs discarded from the outside of the logs I used for lumber making. There is a thick layer of sawdust for insulation in the ceiling.

The hens are moved into their new house at dusk, when they can be easily caught on their perches, and it is not long before they are happily investigating their new territory. I love fresh eggs, but I cannot find the remotest bit of affection for the hens. They go into hysterics at the slightest provocation, and it is always me they accuse with their cold, fishy eyes. Their stupidity amazes me; they love to scratch about in the bare ground underneath my house but hate the soft, deep snow between the two buildings. Although I have beaten a path between our doors, the hens never attempt to use it, preferring to flutter and flap through the unmarked snow. They have also developed a fascination for the Styrofoam insulation beneath my floor. Goodness knows how many holes they have pecked in it. I dread to think what this peculiar diet is doing to the eggs. The bottom of the house will have to be blocked off with shovelled snow. I cannot build a run for the birds until I can afford both chicken wire and the cost of flying it in.

Coastal weather does not usually remain cold for long. Soon, a warm southerly brings wild winds that toss the trees, making them clunk and groan and thrash like cornstalks. Lumps of half-frozen slush slither and crash through the branches. The snow does not melt much on the frozen ground, and under the soggy blanket, scattered in all directions, is my winter's supply of firewood. I haul it by wheelbarrow, three or four huge rounds at a time, and stack it against the house wall under my old blue tarp. The blocks are so wet that when it is cold, they freeze solid and have to be broken apart with a sledgehammer. The wood seems dry enough inside, however, and it burns surprisingly well.

The last job I want to finish before winter is not essential for my survival. Now that the leaves are off the trees, a glitter of water can be seen through the lattice of grey alders on the little island upriver. If I clear them, my horizon will be greatly extended and my view improved. I feel guilty destroying even more bush just for the sake of a view, but I tell myself there are plenty of other alders to house the insects that feed the small birds in the spring. Besides, the flotilla of branches I send bobbing down the river will be appreciated by the beaver at Horseshoe Bend. Now that the sun

takes so long to fight its way through the forest in the morning, I feel a little closed in. I am happier when I can push back my visible boundaries.

When I go out for mail at the end of November, most of Lonesome Lake is frozen, but there is enough open water to discourage me from using the ice. Once again, I have to hunt for the rough trail around the edge. Deer tracks in the snow show me the way across the rock slides, but in the places where there are no marks, the dog always seems to know where to go. The canoe is where I have left it, but a fox has dragged the life jacket away and chewed at it. I tie it in a tree, hoping it will be safe from squirrels. Both the short days and the deteriorating travelling conditions mean that I can no longer do the whole trip during daylight hours, but as most of the bears not already hibernating are upriver feeding on the spawning spring salmon, there is much less risk of meeting them, and I finish my journey by moonlight.

A few days later, I return home. New ice has formed at the foot of Lonesome Lake. It is so transparent, I think it is open water until I realize that the 100 trumpeter swans in the middle of it are not swimming but standing on a firm surface. The sun is going, and the last of its light glows a dull orange on rafts of balloonlike clouds that are faithfully reflected in the perfect mirror of the ice. The swans seem to be walking on an inverted, orange sky.

These birds have excellent eyesight. They start honking the minute I emerge from the trees, although I must be a mile away and the light is very poor. I would probably have failed to notice them at all had it not been for the clamour.

Unlike the swans, I do not trust the new ice, and I take to the trail again. The first part goes over a steep bluff; as I climb it, the swans observe me, continuously bugling in their soft, melodious way, commenting on my progress. As I follow the trail back down again, the volume of trumpeting suddenly increases and the birds panic. There is a deafening roar from 100 pairs of wings and pounding feet, amplified by the thin drum skin of the ice, as the great white birds take off in long, wavering strings and fly up the lake into the dusk. Their mournful crying echoes against the bluffs long after they have passed the limits of my vision. It is one of those moments when time stands still; I cannot move until the purple evening fills the valley and the last melancholy note fades away. I stand on the darkening mountain and think, "No one else has witnessed this. It is mine, and mine alone."

Katie, Dennis and Birch are going to be home at Stuie for Christmas this year, and they have asked me if I would like to go down and join them. Katie loves celebrations. Everyone has a marvellous time at her parties, so it is an invitation that I am delighted to accept.

I have always believed that Christmas without snow is like a turkey without stuffing – perfectly adequate but lacking something. Growing up in England, I remember only one white Christmas; then I moved to the southern hemisphere and spent subsequent holiday seasons crossing the equator in a boat on Lake Victoria, picnicking in the shade of a stand of ghost gums in Australia, making hay in New Zealand (and eating the first new potatoes and peas out of the garden for Christmas dinner) and camping on a wide, white, lonely beach in the Falkland Islands, dining off wild gosling cooked over a fire of horse manure, surrounded by a large and very curious crowd of penguins. Memorable Christmases all, but they did not have snow.

All foreigners know that Canada is buried to the eaves with the white stuff for six months of the year. Before I came to this country, I had looked forward to this winter excitement. But last year, when I wintered at Stuie, I was disappointed to find that by the end of December, the ground was still bare. Where were the blizzards, the whiteouts, the drifts necessitating snowshoes and dogsleds, which had been so vividly described by Jack London and Robert Service and which had inflamed the imagination of my youth? Where were the sparkling crystals, the glittering icicles and snow-laden trees promised so enthusiastically by calendar pictures and postcards? They were certainly not at Stuie. In fact, to add insult to injury, it rained. It poured! Thick, black clouds choked the valley, shutting out the mountains and making dripping tunnels of the trees. Apart from anything else, without snow on the ground, it was impossible to find my way to the outhouse in the dark without tripping over stumps and walking into wet, overhanging branches on the way. I was appalled. I thought with longing of those other Christmases I had so casually consigned to the past, of the smells of eucalyptus and curing hay and the audiences of sharp-eyed and gossiping penguins. If I stayed in Canada, was I doomed forever to these wet and dreary winters?

But so far this year, winter has been everything I desire. The sky during December has been cold and clear, and the sun sparkles on a fairy-tale frosting of snow. As I hike out to Stuie, I have my first taste of walking on the ice, an experience both thrilling and nerve-racking. I am very conscious of that fragile skin, the tenuous membrane that separates me from, at best, an unpleasant dunking. My apprehension is not helped by the terrifying pings, cracks, whines, groans and subterranean gurgles that issue from beneath my feet. But I am not complaining; this is winter as it should be. My elongated, purple shadow points ahead of me, down the blinding, creamy, snow-covered ice; Robert Service's "Dog-nosed mountains bay at the moon" (or they would were it not the middle of the day). Is it too irreverent, I wonder, to categorize the ice's monstrous attack of flatulence under "The Call of the Wild"?

The snow, however, is not very deep. Knobby rocks poke through on the trail between the two lakes, and by the foot of the Stillwater, bare patches of ground are showing beneath the trees. It is noticeably warmer, and the sky is beginning to film over with cloud. Then comes the wearying slog along the tote road; it is dark when I arrive at the highway by the bottom of The Hill. Dirty snow lies piled up by the roadside, but the road itself is bare, and it gleams faintly with a sheen of drizzle.

Katie and Dennis have driven my truck up this far—a welcome surprise. The hood is still faintly warm, so it has not been here long. By the time I reach Stuie, the night is as black and thick as soot and it is raining again.

So I do not have a white Christmas after all. But on the night of the 25th, as I stumble to the outhouse in the dripping dark, getting slapped in the face by trailing, sodden cedar branches on the way, I think of the warmth between the old log walls of the house, of the tree, the lights, the exciting crackle of Christmas paper, the smell of food and the wonderful circle of smiling faces, and I know it does not really matter. Who needs snow at Christmas when you have all the rest?

A day or two later, I set off for home. The temperature has dropped again, and as I head upriver, I walk back into a world of white. I start as early as I can, but day is ending when I reach Lonesome Lake, and the sky is pink and milky with mare's tails. The upper part of the lake is always tricky with patches of open water, so when it grows too dark to see properly, I hike to a point of land and scratch about for the makings of a fire. I smash lumps of ice with the axe to fill the billy and crouch around the flickering sticks. The moon is a day past full, and it will rise in an hour: it will give me all the light I will need.

Supper is soup and tea and turkey sandwiches that taste of smoke where they have been thawed too close to the flames. The warm spell of the past few days has encouraged large crystals to form on the ice, some long like needles, some in the forms of feather fans and others in a series of hexagonal plates. As the moon rises, they flash like fairy fire and the mountains sail moon-white against an indigo sky.

Chapter 15
The Trumpeters

Lonesome Lake is famous for its trumpeter swans. In his early days in the valley, Ralph Edwards hired himself out as a guide to a grizzly hunter who was astounded to recognize these rare birds at Lonesome Lake. At one time, they thrived all over North America, even as far south and east as Florida. But their quills were valued as pens and their down for powder puffs; the Hudson's Bay Company exported thousands of skins. Their size, with a wingspan of eight feet, their whiteness and their inability to adapt quickly to changes soon drove them to the border of extinction. In 1932, when the Canadian Wildlife Service heard about this pocket of survivors, it worked with Ralph to institute the Lonesome Lake Trumpeter Swan Feeding Programme. While Trudy was still a child, she took over the job, and she has been doing it ever since. Instead of the handful of birds that used to winter here, there are sometimes as many as 400. Other wintering grounds in previously unknown coastal inlets, along with their nesting areas in Alaska, have also been discovered, and the future of the West Coast population seems a lot more secure.

A swan, with its snowy plumage and long neck, has long been a symbol of elegance, but being the world's largest freshwater fowl means that the trumpeter also has one of the world's largest pairs of webbed feet. In flight, they are flattened under the tail, and in the water, although very efficient as paddlers and mud stirrers, they are hidden and do not detract from the image of gracefulness. But on land, they are an embarrassment.

A swan's feet are black, webbed and as big as a side plate, with claws on the toes to help the bird scramble out of the water. They turn inward – so much so that they often overlap – and support two thick, short, leathery legs, slightly bowed. When the bird comes down from the sky, the great feet are flung forward to reduce speed, but this cannot stop the swan from sliding like an aircraft across the ice, colliding with any other birds unfortunate enough to be in the way. At such times, there is great gabbling and tail wagging until dignity is restored.

The swans start arriving in small groups during October, and they work the weedy shallows on the lakes and river, grubbing about in the mud for roots. They cannot dive, and their feeding areas are therefore limited to water of no greater depth than the length of their necks. When the shallow areas freeze, the swans congregate daily at Lonesome Lake, flying low in long, undulating ribbons of winking wings, to receive the government-sponsored grain allowance as a supplement to their foraging.

Every day, from freeze-up until early March, when the birds begin to head north, someone – usually Trudy, although now that I am here, I sometimes go down as well – hikes down to the grain shed at the far end of the lagoon by the wharf. There, the river channel passes close to the shore, and except in very cold spells, the swans can be fed in the water. As soon as we step onto the ice half a mile away, the chorus of trumpeting swells and many of the birds take off to meet us. Squadrons of wild, honking swans fly past at eye level, their wings whooshing and their pinion feathers rattling as they swerve in synchrony to avoid us.

Once feeding has started in the fall, the birds become accustomed to us. It is quite something to stand in the middle of 400 giant swans. Their beaks are waist-high and only inches from our heads as we bend to scoop grain from the sacks. The clamour becomes deafening, then suddenly muffled as the heads dive into the water. The grain swishes through the air and patters onto the densely packed backs; some of the beaks clatter on the edge of the ice as the swans pick up spilled morsels.

When the river is frozen, the swans have to feed off the ice, and they can do this only if the surface is firm. If it has snowed, the sack of grain has to be carried back and forth, the trumpeting flock in pursuit, until a large enough feeding area has been flattened by 400 pairs of those wonderful black feet.

Half a pound of barley per bird per day means that up to 14,000 pounds of grain have to be brought in annually. It used to be horsepacked and rafted up the lakes, an enormously time-consuming chore that could take six weeks, but now, it is flown in from Nimpo. The Turners organize the flights, and they stagger them throughout the year so that their mail can

be flown in with the grain. As we have no means of communicating with the floatplane base and they, naturally, cannot contact us, bookings are made weeks ahead by mail in the hope that the weather, the pilot and the plane will all cooperate. Most of the time, the system works, but plane days can sometimes be the peak of frustration.

When I was out at Christmas, I booked a flight for my own supplies on December 30. Precious money has been reserved for this occasion. Not only am I expecting a variety of food and much-needed clothes and boots, but I am also looking forward to receiving all kinds of personal possessions – books, ornaments and the other detritus of my life – completely useless to anyone else but items that I have not quite been able to part with.

At the appointed time, 10 a.m., I am down at the lagoon. Cloud cover is low, so I light a fire and wait. Four hours later, the clouds lift out of the valley, although they still hang about the peaks: it is possible that Nimpo is not yet clear. Without a phone or radio, there is no way to find out why the pilot does not come. When the light fails, I pack up and go home.

The next day is foggy again, but although it clears around noon, by the end of the day, the plane still has not arrived. I have a very painful bout of tonsillitis – a Christmas gift I could well have done without. Sitting on the ice is not helping it any. So I leave the outgoing mail wrapped in plastic, under a tripod of poles decked with bright orange survey ribbons, hoping that the pilot will see it. The weather remains reasonable for a week, but there is no plane. One night, a tremendous warm wind springs up and beats my house with shuddering gusts. In the morning, it is pouring with rain. The mail is still sitting on the ice. By noon, it is snowing, huge white flakes tumbling thick and fast, each window a dazzling blur. At first, it is too warm for the snow to accumulate, but by evening, it is deepening, heavy wet stuff that bows and breaks the birches and slithers with solid thumps off the firs. I fear for my roof: the long, shallow south side has not been well designed for such conditions. I get up in the night and shovel all I can reach from the ladder—it is too slippery to try to walk up top. By morning, the snow is 14 inches deep, and it is raining again.

It rains for days, packing the snow to icy slush and turning the surface of the lagoon to soup. On Sunday, January 12, the sky is clear, but the warm wind still roars and mare's tails stream across the mountains from the west. Several times, we hear planes of all sizes, for when the weather is bad on the coast, aircraft often use our long, north-south valley as a skyway. The sun leaves us, but it still shines on the peaks when a red Cessna flies low overhead and dips toward the lake. I grab my pack and hike on down. The plane, which has been and gone by the time I get there, has carved a channel through the thin new ice on top of the soup; beside it, shrouded in my blue tarp, is a small pile of freight. It is only half a load— no doubt the pilot worried about the poor conditions—but the urgent things like food have come. The rest will have to wait at Nimpo until finances permit another flight. There is no indication as to why the pilot did not come before the weather broke.

The next day, it is raining again. I move the freight off the ice for fear it will be frozen in if the weather ever turns cold again. The trail is far too icy for the horses, and all the loads have to be carefully backpacked home over treacherous footing. I figure it is high time the dog earns her keep, so she has to pack too. She hates it. Her ears and tail droop every time she sees her saddlebags. She tries to creep under bushes and hide. But I praise her constantly, and she becomes at least resigned to it. Wearing a most martyred expression, she plods valiantly behind.

It is a strange collection of items that eventually finds its way into that remote corner of the wilderness. There is the huge, clay water pot from Afghanistan that I did not really want, but the man sitting beside the dusty road took a 10-Afghani note from my hand and started to give me mountains of change—the pot cost one-tenth of a cent. I dragged it all across Asia and the Antipodes; it is now being backpacked over a frozen trail in British Columbia. Then there are the shells from the South Sea Islands, brought to me by the children in the palm-fringed villages where I stayed, with memories of an environment that could hardly be more different from the place where I am now living. There is the great, round bell from the cow I milked one summer in Switzerland, a water gourd from Uganda, burned with a design of dark loops and swirls, and a model reed boat from Lake Titicaca. There is a pinecone from a monkey puzzle tree in Chile and a penguin egg from the Falkland Islands, as well as a box of old bottles of watery green glass that I dug out of a dump there. And there are books, books and more books. The dog is the only one who does not appreciate my library, for she is the one who has to carry it.

All these things have travelled long and strange journeys, and they have now come together in the house that I have built. Within these log walls is the history of my life.

Chapter 16

Freeze-Up

We have one really cold spell in February: the temperature drops to minus 22 degrees F. That is when I discover the inadequacy of my floor insulation. The more the stove roars, the more the wind howls through the gaps between the uneven floorboards. Everything more than a few feet away from the stove freezes solid. The water bucket, which is a five-gallon plastic pail, buckles with heat from the stove on one side but retains a lump of ice on the other. Eggs, when cracked on the side of the pan, drop into the fat with a wooden clunk and have a strange, gritty texture when eaten. The drafts around the badly fitting window frames can be blocked with wool (for I have a couple of fleeces that I hope to spin), but I can do little about the floor. The rock-hard snow that remains after the winter thaws is not sufficient to bank the walls. I have to wear two pairs of long johns, my goose-down coat, gloves and a hat to keep warm inside the house; I do not remove my outdoor clothes for a week.

An ice dam forms at Horseshoe Bend. The water behind it backs up and rises five feet, coming close to the top of the bank by the house and spilling over the lower meadows across the river. It solidifies into patterns of frozen swirls, each little ridge decorated with spiky crystals. The familiar rushing chatter of the river is suddenly silenced.

By the house, the ice is 14 inches thick, but it is slush ice, full of air pockets and unsafe to walk on. Every day, I rechop a hole by the bank to fetch water. Some of the ice formations are spectacular. Just above the little island is a hole that never freezes, and through it, water constantly spurts like molten rock from a volcano. It flows away from the vent and congeals like green lava; the centre of the river is soon noticeably higher than the edges. Wraiths of frost smoke issue from the hole, shot through with gold during the two brief hours of sun that are all the narrow valley allows us at this time of year.

South of the property, a tangle of fallen trees has formed dams and canyons of ice, glazed with crystals where the frost smoke drifts through. Where the water has splashed up, they are hung with frills of rounded icicles swollen at the bottom and fringed with little knobs. Living in this world of fairy grottoes is an amazing creature called the water ouzel. This dark, thrushlike bird looks anything but aquatic, and yet it flings itself from the ice shelf into the river, where it walks along the bottom, grasping stones with its long toes, looking for insect larvae. It pops to the surface like a cork, whizzes about like a whirligig, then flutters back onto the ice and bobs with the jerky rhythm that has earned it its common name of "dipper." These birds are very territorial. The three or four who live close to the house squabble furiously if one encroaches on another's property. On sunny days, they sing: the waterfall of trills and warbles must rank them among the world's best songsters. It is the kind of rich performance normally associated with spring, and it is all the more delightful and amazing to hear it in such harsh, wintry conditions.

Cleaning clothes in cold weather presents problems. Washing them is easy enough, for it is not much of a chore to haul water to the tub on the stove and heat it. But heavy wool garments need thorough rinsing, and the quickest way to do it is to hang them on the end of a long stick and dunk them through the ice hole into the river. At first, I dropped them beside the hole onto the ice shelf to drain, but they stuck at once and ripped when I tried to pull them free. So I have learned to lean the stiffening garments against the woodpile, then bring them into the house a few at a time, rigid as boards, until I can thaw them sufficiently to bend them and hang them over the rack to drip.

When the temperature rises to minus 4 degrees F, it feels positively tropical. Coats and gloves are shed, even outside (after all, at my house, outside temperatures are not much different from those inside). The ice jam at Horseshoe Bend goes out, and the water level drops, leaving the riverbed by the bank high and dry. I now have a chest-deep hole, surrounded by a 14-inch thickness of ice, with nothing but air underneath. The centre of the river has sagged to water level, and the angle from the bank is far too steep to walk on, even if I thought it was safe. I have to use a sledgehammer to pound a route to open water. The warmth soon breaks up

the river, and it finds its voice again. Floes bump and grate until the main channel is clear, and the water makes curious, sucking slaps under the remaining shelf.

Just before Christmas, the Turners butchered Valerian. She was still in her prime but repeatedly failed to conceive, and they decided to make room for one of the heifers who would soon calve. This means there is plenty of fresh beef, and I am able to purchase half the carcass. I keep most of it in the Turners' meat safe, a screened, shady, well-ventilated room in one of their heavy log outbuildings. Periodically, I bring a 50-pound lump over to my house and hang it from the jutting end of a ceiling joist against my north wall. One day, I hear an odd thumping as if someone is beating the wall on the outside. Suspecting the cat or dog of trying to get at the meat, I shut them up, but the thumping continues. I creep outside and stand quietly by the corner of the house. After a few minutes, the neat, bright eyes, pointy nose and furry, rounded ears of a marten appear from under the wall. He runs up the logs and hangs on the swinging leg of beef, using his weight to tear off a mouthful as he drops to the snow. I manage to foil his efforts, but he continues to hang about, an intelligent and inquisitive animal. He peers from the holes in the woodpile or leaps daintily through the snow, and I have grown quite fond of him.

Many other animals share the winter with us. Wolf tracks are common. Sometimes, the valley rings with wolfsong, a lament so stirring and mysterious, it seems to emphasize the gulf between humans and our fellow creatures. I have seen these fabled animals only once, while hiking above the timberline during the summer before I started building. There were three of them, scouting the pockets of snow below me for mice. Distant as they were, seeing them was an unforgettable thrill, and I long to see more of them.

A fox comes nightly to pick over the bones that the dog has scattered. The cat always announces the fox's presence by growling on the porch, and I waken to see the pretty, bushy-tailed animal standing light-footed in the moonlight. One night, I hear a heavy crunching and am surprised to see a moose right under the window, for the few that winter in the area usually stay down at the lagoon. Scraps of fat wired to a tree attract squirrels, Steller's jays, whisky-jacks and that wily character and great conversationalist, the raven. Most of the wildlife is present here because of the open water in the river. Eagles hunch like vultures on bare branches against the sky, and groups of otters coil through the water in such a swift procession of heads and bodies, it is impossible to count them. They snort and growl from the caverns beneath the ice shelf, following me as I walk upon it, surfacing in air pockets beneath my feet and snarling fearsomely only inches away from my boots, making my toes curl.

Families of swans work the river at times, but there is little feed there. They churn furiously with their feet, then duck their heads to filter the delicacies from the mud. Mergansers bob about for the small aquatic animals disturbed by the swans' paddling, but these slim, crested ducks risk an occasional tweak from a swan's beak for their temerity.

People from the city wonder how those of us who live in the bush survive without laid-on entertainment. There are no social gatherings and no television; even radio reception leaves much to be desired. Some California stations come through at night, but the constant silly advertising is too irritating to put up with. CBC, if I can raise it at all, fades out during daylight hours, but in the winter, I can usually hear the news at both ends of the day. It comes from Vancouver, and the advice to avoid a traffic snarl on Lion's Gate Bridge or to take an umbrella to work seems irrelevant.

Unfortunately, the media feel it is necessary to sell news like a soap opera. To hear bits of news on days of poor reception is worse than hearing no news at all. Once, I caught the faint announcement that there would be an extended broadcast at 7 a.m. because . . . I could not hear why. The speaker's voice was full of tension; as the CBC had done a similar thing a month before when the space shuttle *Challenger* exploded, I wondered what earth-shattering disaster had happened this time. I waited, ear close to the set, for the next news, but at 7 o'clock, the radio was silent. The following morning, I picked up something about a crash, but everything else was indistinct. The announcer's voice still rang with passion. What kind of a crash could be so important? A plane crash? Had a jumbo jet crash-landed on a heavily populated area, killing thousands? Had a political crash sparked an incident that had put us on the brink of nuclear war? I began to feel worried. What *had* happened? Two days later, reception came through clear and strong. A train had derailed in northern Alberta, killing 20 people. No doubt it was tragic for those involved, but hardly material, I thought, for such a sensational delivery.

The mainstay of my intellectual life is the mail-order library. It is a marvellous service. The government pays the postage both ways, and I often have up to 60 books for two or three months at a time. They are sent to the Turners' address at Nimpo Lake, and they come in on the planes with the swan grain. A huge computer printout of popular titles is sent to subscribers, but I prefer specialized material and have made long lists of requests. The lady in the head office scours all the libraries throughout the interior of British Columbia: books come to me from Quesnel, Lillouette, Williams Lake, Hundred Mile and many smaller communities. If the librarian, whom I know simply as Marcia, cannot find what I want, she substitutes anything similar and throws a few more in for good measure. Plane days are like Christmas, for I never know what I will find in the parcels. The bulk of my requests are related to my work as an artist; the books are my teachers and my art galleries, and I have learned tremendously from them.

By February, the days are noticeably longer and the temperatures warmer. The remaining meat has to be preserved, and life revolves around that hissing, snorting monster, the pressure canner. There is horsemeat to deal with, as well as beef. Feed is short, and Ginger, who has never worked well in harness, had to go. It is a hard thing to kill a healthy animal that you have worked with for years, but it was out of the question to bring feed in from outside, and all the animals would suffer if she were allowed to live. One morning, a shot rings out across the river, and I know she is gone. Independence brings its own penalties.

The dark, dry horseflesh is trimmed of its yellow fat, cut up and boiled, then ground and dried for dog food. It is a tedious business, and as my stove space is limited, the day has to be carefully planned. I can beef by day, boil horsemeat at night and grind it on my dimly lit kitchen bench before the sun rises in the morning. The mincer makes an unpleasant, gristly sound. I feel as though I am committed to some Stygian task, endlessly grinding flesh by lamplight.

Chapter 17

Spring Fever

Winter travel is rarely quiet—snow crunches or squeaks with every footfall—and this time, successive rains and frosts have created layers of paper-thin ice in air pockets above the main surface of Lonesome Lake. Each step is accompanied by the shattering discord of breaking glass—like seven miles of walking through cold frames.

And then it is March. The icy remains of the snow are slow to depart, and the thick slabs of ice left high and dry on the banks after the river thawed are little changed. Although the sun is glorious at times, the winds are brisk and cool, and the nights sharp with frost. The swans left abruptly after the cold spell in February; only a few early, smaller summer migrants have arrived. They make an occasional attempt to sing, but their efforts are mere tokens. Inside the house, big, black flies emerge from nowhere and buzz and batter against the sealed windows.

It is a restless time, too cold to work out-of-doors and too bright to stay inside. The building debris in the yard is a shock as the snow recedes, but little can be done with it until the ground thaws. Gardening is out of the question, but I sow seeds for cabbages, onions and tomatoes in plastic gallon chain-oil containers with their sides cut off; these unlovely containers crowd my sunniest windowsills. I drool at the thought of fresh greens, still so many weeks away. I bring twigs of cottonwood and alder into the house:

the alder catkins elongate immediately and shed pools of pollen over the floor, but the cottonwood buds open slowly, filling the room with their incomparable fragrance.

My friend the marten is an opportunist. He notices the softening of the ground before I do, and one day, he digs beneath the grizzly-proof walls of my henhouse and kills two birds. He would probably have got the lot if the chickens' hysterics had not confused him and alerted me: their irritating screeching and fluttering have a purpose after all. The marten wisely abandons his victims when I arrive, so I think I might as well put them in the pot for myself. Chicken meat is a treat for me, but the hens are a laying breed. There is hardly a mouthful on them, and they would have been a lot more use to me as egg producers. I hack at the ground around the chicken house and manage to put in posts to hold the chicken wire that came in on a February plane. I spread some of the wire horizontally at the base of the fence and weight it with rocks to prevent further unwanted excavations.

At this time of year, the mule deer become bold. They seem to have little fear of me. They congregate in the clearing to nibble at the tiny spikes of new, green, colonizing weeds, and I can walk openly about the house and yard without disturbing them. Provided I do not move too quickly, they stare at me with only the mildest curiosity before dropping their heads again. At first, they are more interested in the dog, but although she watches them continuously, she obediently leaves them alone and they learn to ignore her too. This apparent tameness will last for several weeks, until the herd separates at the end of May when the does drop their fawns.

One of the deer that come into the clearing receives a very nasty shock. I have just finished the chicken run, and the three remaining hens are dust bathing in the early spring sunshine. Along comes the mule deer, poking alone and without concern, through the forest. As she passes close to the hens, she suddenly sees them. She stops dead, snorts and jerks her head forward, ears as rigid as table-tennis paddles — the classic picture of absolute astonishment. No way is she going any nearer to those peculiar animals. She commences a wide detour, never taking her eyes off the birds. She is so comically absorbed in them, every muscle of her body quivering with attention, that she does not see me standing beside the house, directly in her path. I wait until she is almost close enough to touch, until I can resist it no longer. "Boo!" I say. The deer jumps at least four feet off the ground; way up against the base of the mountain, she is still running.

Now that the days are no longer spent single-mindedly trying to get a roof over my head, I can begin to investigate my surroundings. Along the steep sides of the valley, the forest thins, and it is easy to walk through. But in places, pockets of lodgepole pine, killed long ago by the bark beetle, are a jumble of rotting windfalls. One day, I scramble to the top of the valley. Above the western rim, I can see the summits of the mountains that surround the plateau behind Hunlen Falls. Along the Atnarko, two lakes are visible upriver; Lonesome Lake, below the homestead, is scarred with dark patches of rotten ice and open water. The expanded horizon is good for my restlessness, and the walk soon becomes a favourite of mine. Sometimes the valley is filled with fog, and I can climb through it into the sunshine.

April has come, and the snow has finally disappeared. The ice has gone out from the lake, but cold winds keep spring at bay. The seedlings on my windowsills are sickly and stunted; it is too cold for them there, but closer to the stove, there is not enough light.

I have been looking forward to my first trip in the canoe; I imagine my craft sliding into the water and drifting effortlessly down a motionless lake, so much more pleasant than the wearying scramble on the trail around the edge. But when I go to town at the end of the month, a wild southerly is blowing. At first, it is exhilarating to be pushed so easily over the roller-coaster waves, but at the north end of the lake, where the wind has increased the power of the waves, I become frightened. Whitecaps hiss down the grey-green shoulders of water. The canoe bobs like a duck, and I dare not turn it broadside to the waves; I find it increasingly difficult to choose a course. The section from the last point to the outlet is always the most dangerous when the wind is from this direction. Visualizing the water crashing onto the rocky beach where I usually land, I do not know if the canoe will survive it. I am still a couple of miles from the foot of the lake, but when I find a tiny pocket of sand sandwiched between rocks on the shoreline, I steer for it and leap into knee-deep water in my socks, hauling the canoe quickly over drift logs before it can be damaged or swamped.

The spits of wind-driven rain turn to snow. At the Stillwater, a thin covering of slush on the ground makes the wet roots and rocks extremely slippery. On the tote road, the snow is two inches deep and falling thick and fast. There is no one to meet me. My coat leaks, and I am soaked through. No matter how hard I walk, pounding my feet on the stony ground, I cannot get warm. Some food might help—I've had nothing to eat all day—but I am so cold, I dare not stop to pull the sandwiches out of my pack.

It is dusk when I reach the highway. I have been travelling continuously for 10 hours and still have 12 miles to go to reach Stuie. Hitchhiking is surely out of the question, for no one will attempt The Hill in this weather; it will have snowed much more heavily up there. My only hope is that Katie or Dennis might drive up the road after dark, as they often do when they know I am coming.

But no sooner do I set foot on the highway than I hear a vehicle pull to a stop behind me. The driver is from Alaska. Sure, he says, he had to

wait for the plough at the top of The Hill, but such conditions hold no terrors for him. In 20 minutes, I am seated by a roaring fire at Stuie with a hot mug of tea.

The storm is the last of the winter. The wild gooseberry, always one of the earliest plants to flower, springs suddenly into leaf. The young bull moose, which startled me beneath my window during the winter and which I have encountered several times down at the lagoon, begins to grow his new horns. They are horizontal sticks with knobs on the end that protrude from his head like the antennae of some extraterrestrial being.

May brings a chance to earn some money. During the winter, Katie and Dennis and their three nearest neighbours have acquired electricity. To offset the high cost of extending the power line for 12 miles, they elected to do much of the work themselves. The right-of-way has been cleared, and the poles planted and hooked up, but a lot of brush still lies by the roadside; part of the contract is to cart it away. Spring is a busy time for anyone connected with the tourist business, so I have been hired to do the job.

I am no stranger to brush clearing and do not imagine that the work will be pleasant, but there are compensations. There can be few places more beautiful than the Bella Coola Valley in spring. Birches fountain with golden catkins, and the little stunted aspens that grow on the rock slides are decorated with coppery leaves as bright and round as new pennies. The birds, which have been waiting so long in the wings, perform their seasonal symphony: varied thrushes ring like telephone bells, blue grouse boom through inflated throat sacs, and ruffed grouse putter like little gas motors as they beat the air with their wings. Pileated woodpeckers drum sonorous rolls against dead snags, and sapsuckers rattle a catchy little rhythm like something out of Walt Disney. Chickadees sing their summer song, robins scuttle across the grass like mice, and hummingbirds whiz and flash their iridescent jewellery in the sunlight.

Towering clouds form and boil and rip apart about Mount Stupendous' multiple summits, and avalanches roar down its rocky ramparts. The trees are a glory of spring green that lasts for weeks, wildflowers star the roadside, and skunk cabbages glow like yellow lanterns in the dark cedar swamps. Black bears feast on these, and I see them often.

But when I arrive for work, I find the pristine beauty shattered. Heavy machinery works the base of the mountains, and enormous explosions shake their very foundations as a logging company blasts a road. The Talchako River, which divides the mountains from the highway, is also the boundary of Tweedsmuir Park. This means that the spectacular mountains on the other side of the valley are unprotected. Chain saws whine, and the dull crump of falling trees, audible for miles, sounds like the distant boom of heavy artillery. The scars of destruction spread swiftly up the sides of the valley like the scabrous sores of an incurable disease. After horrified protests from residents, the logging company said it would landscape smaller blocks in future, but it does not seem to make much difference. For generations, these eyesores will be a monument to human greed.

Clear-cut logging is devastating to an environment, especially on a steep mountainside. The so-called trash is bulldozed together and burned, and the thin, poor soil, which takes centuries to form in a slowly growing fir forest, is often burned as well. Where heavy rains along the coast do not wash away the soil that is left, the forest will grow again. But the drier areas need replanting. This is not always done, and even if it is, nothing can survive where the soil has been destroyed. The unprotected slopes are quick to erode, and silt fouls the river, deoxygenating the water and suffocating the eggs of the spawning salmon. Very little life in this part of the world, human or otherwise, is not somehow involved with the salmon's cycle; if that is affected, the food chain is soon disrupted.

If the forest does regenerate, the logging companies spray the fast-sprouting willows and alders that nature has placed to protect the soil and provide nutrients from their quickly decaying leaves. The chemicals, which we are assured are "safe," are flushed down the eroding hillsides into the river. "Economy! Economy!" cry the loggers, and the politicians echo, "Economy!" in reply. But what will happen to the economy when there are no more trees left to cut, when one of the world's most important Pacific salmon spawning grounds is destroyed, when roads allow hunters easy access to areas previously protected by their inaccessibility and when the tourists, who are lured by the "unspoiled beauty" of the valley, turn away in disgust?

Chapter 18
Cat Tales

My cat has been making a nuisance of herself with my neighbours, especially when she is in heat, which seems to be most of the time. She yowls most horribly and spends all her time across the river beating up the Turners' cats (also female); the Turners' patience is understandably wearing thin. So as the vet comes to Bella Coola four times a year and as one of his visits coincides with my brush-clearing job, I have brought the cat out with me to be spayed.

She has always been feisty, with a mind of her own. I put her into a sack inside a box and tie her onto my backpack, not expecting her to enjoy it but hoping she will be sufficiently confused to stay there. Within two miles, she fights her way out, and I have to carry her in my arms. She growls in frustration all the way and sometimes tries to leap up a tree, but I have a string around her neck and am able to catch her again without any trouble. When she was still a kitten in the camp, she tried to follow me when I was working with the chain saw; for her own protection, I broke her to a collar and leash. She fought it, at first, but came to accept it surprisingly well, which was a blessing on the journey out, particularly in the canoe. Poor thing, she hates the water and digs her claws into my thighs as I kneel and paddle, but she does not try to escape. Finally, at the end of the trail, she suffers the further indignity of being put back into the sack on the floor of the truck, which must frighten her greatly.

At Stuie, I usually stay in a cabin that belongs to the previous owner of Katie and Dennis's property. He seldom uses the place, and Katie and Dennis park odd visitors in the cabin in return for maintaining it. It is a large, ranch-style house made of machine-cut cedar only four inches thick. It has enormous windows that frame the magnificent view, but the building is far from practical most of the year. Permanently fastened, shop-sized panes of glass face south to accommodate the panorama. In summer, the place is like an oven: the few windows that open are not sufficient to ventilate the building. It is impossible to heat in winter, and the plumbing has been so poorly designed that it cannot be properly drained; the pipes always pop apart in the spring. The foundations are merely perched on the ground, and frost heaves have moved them so much that the building has warped. Few of the doors close properly.

But it has one redeeming feature: it looks great. The large expanse of well-lit, oiled cedar walls is a flattering place to display my paintings, so for the summer, I turn the main room into a small art gallery.

Pussy Cat is given the run of the place, with a litter box in the utility room. She is a good mouser and will earn her keep. In the kitchen is a wood stove, and because the plumbing is not fixed, a five-gallon drum of water stands on the counter. When I leave for work the first morning, I lock the two doors, something we do not usually do, but I do not want someone to walk in and forget about the cat. The locked door might remind them. Pussy Cat does not like strangers, and after the upsets of the journey, she could easily escape and go wild. There are enough male cats about to start a population explosion, which would be a disaster to the smaller wildlife.

The cabin is out of sight of Katie and Dennis's house, where I clean myself up and dine that evening. Katie and Dennis are not at home, but their dog, a sister to mine, is on the porch. Soon, the dogs bark their bear bark: sure enough, they have treed a black bear across the yard. I call them off and shut them up, hoping that the bear will go away. Tucked under the cedars that fill the property are several rental cabins, unoccupied at the moment, although one has only just been vacated. The bear climbs down the tree and heads straight for it; no doubt, the smell of food or garbage still lingers. The bear stands on his hind legs and methodically pushes against all the windows, first ripping the screens carefully with his claws. I go outside and yell at him, hoping to scare him off, but he simply turns and glowers at me. I retreat rather helplessly into the house and watch. He is unable to get into the cabin, and he eventually loses interest and walks away. He seems totally cabin-oriented, for he ignores a stack of empty garbage cans close by, usually the first target for scavenging bears. As I have not heard of any problem bears in the area, I assume he has been a nuisance elsewhere and has been trapped and released in the park in the hope that he will mend his ways, a ploy that is only sometimes successful.

Just before dark, I walk up to my lodging and unlock the back door. We do not have a key for the front one; it has been locked from the inside. The dogs, who accompanied me across the property, are barking frantically, so the bear must be very close. I step along the hall, walk into the main room – and stop in horror. The furniture has been tipped upside down and thrown all over the place. It has to be the bear.

By this time, Dennis is home, and I bolt back down the hill to fetch him and the shotgun. When we return, the cabin is empty. The front door, which I had never even looked at on my way to the back of the cabin, is wide open, and so is the kitchen window. The lock obviously did not catch properly in the warped doorframe; it is easy to imagine the bear pushing it and walking in. He must have found the cat. She apparently dived under the heavy couch, for it was tossed aside and the piles of cushions were strewn everywhere. Strangely, nothing is ripped. Pussy Cat must have then fled under the stove, for that was the next thing to go over. The water container had followed – its contents made a glorious mud pie with the soot and ashes from the stove. The bear trampled through it, then continued to charge around the building after the cat. His black, greasy paw marks are everywhere – all over the furniture and high up the walls.

It could be much worse. Nothing is broken or seriously damaged except the firebox door of the stove, which was crushed as it fell. Bears defecate frequently and copiously when scared, but this one has not done so, which again shows his familiarity with buildings. My second thought – the first was for the cat – is for the paintings hung all around the walls, but miraculously, only one is damaged. The paper is not torn, but right down the centre of it are five deep claw marks. There are many stories about animals that have been used to enhance or create artworks, but I don't think anyone has used a bear before. On the cover of a book of press clippings is a wonderful black paw print that, fortunately, won't wipe off. As for Pussy Cat, I never expect to see her again, for I have looked everywhere for her. But after I double-check the doors and prepare for bed, there is a small meow, and a very frightened animal jumps onto my sleeping bag. Where she managed to hide, I cannot begin to guess.

The bear hangs about for several days. The conservation officer and the park ranger are both away, so they cannot deal with it. One night, at 4 a.m., the bear tries to break into the fishing lodge next door and is shot.

When the cat has recovered from her operation, we return home. Once again, the seasons have turned with a rush, and travelling conditions have changed dramatically. The late, cold spring followed by a sudden hot spell has flushed the snow from the mountains, and the creeks are in full flood. Near the start of the tote road, the usual washout is scoured into a deep, roaring gully that cannot be crossed by a vehicle. For about a mile after this, the river is two feet deep over the rutted track. I leave the truck by the washout (Katie and Dennis will come up later and fetch it), and clutching Pussy Cat in my arms, I wade into the water. The cat goes berserk. With a frantic yowl, she digs her claws into my face and tries to climb on top of my head. There is nothing for it but to force her struggling body into the sack and hang on. She growls and moans every step of the way through the water. I expect to be wet above the knees numerous times during the day, so it will not likely be a very pleasant journey.

The forest between the lakes is a maelstrom of roaring water. Part of the Atnarko must have changed course, for swift channels flow in completely new places. Many are too deep and too fast to walk through, and I have to hunt up and down for footlogs. Hunlen Creek is awesome. White waters crash over the boulders; the footlogs I usually use are either washed away or buried under the torrent. Fortunately, upstream, where the worst channel has been forced into two streams around a pile of rocks, two slim poles seem to provide a route. Loosening the waist belt of my pack and clutching Pussy Cat firmly in her sack, I climb onto the pole that crosses the first and worst part of the channel—if I can cope with this one, the other side will be easy. The pole does not look safe, for it is a partially rotten fir only six inches through, but the alternative is to turn back to the Stillwater and hike the long way home via the tourist trail to Hunlen Falls. This is not a bad trip in itself, but it would take two days, and with Pussy Cat, it would be miserable. So the footlog seems the best solution. If I think about it too much, I will never dare attempt it. So I concentrate on my feet and try to forget the water. In 10 swift steps, I am across. Pussy Cat is so frightened, she doesn't even squeak.

Poor animal. She has one more mishap before she is back on home ground. As I step out of the canoe at the head of Lonesome Lake, she jumps too. I have not yet untied her, so her string brings her up short and she lands—plop—in the water. Will she ever forgive me?

Chapter 19

Summer in the High Country

With my hard-earned money, I can buy more supplies and fly them in. I now have a new bar for the chain saw, and my first job is to cut more boards to build shelves and tables. I install an extra window in the dark corner by the stove, then I cut heavy planks, 26 feet long, to nail onto the porch for decking. It will soon be time for the cows to graze this side of the river, so the next job is to surround the yard with a cowproof fence. The problem of the inadequate floor insulation needs addressing, and I struggle under a tiny crawlspace to try to put in another layer. I build a woodshed and construct a lean-to against the house to store tools and meat. I butcher up the logs and stumps remaining in the clearing, then rake up the chips and sawdust and burn the piles a little at a time, very carefully. Small plants are beginning to colonize the clearing: dandelions, corydalis, wild roses and the suckers of birch and cottonwood. The whole place is looking less raw and more civilized.

The garden that the Turners ploughed up for me on the other side of the river is in a hollow and naturally subirrigated, but being low, it is the first place to succumb to a frost. My house site is perhaps a foot or two higher, which makes it a little warmer; the closeness to the water also probably helps modify the temperature. It would seem logical to grow the tender plants close to the house, but here, there is almost no soil; the ground is merely coarse granite gravel full of rocks and a little dark dust. When the Turners first cleared their property, they scattered grass seed under the trees to find out which areas would be productive. My house site proved barren, which is why they gave it to me. Good growing land is in such short supply that none of it can be used for other purposes. I will have to bring my soil from elsewhere.

Every year at high water, the river partially submerges the little island in front of the house, washing alluvium into pockets between rock and root. I backpack this by the bucketload across a big fir footlog that connects the island to the bank and dump it into the wheelbarrow to bring it the rest of the way. I build little rectangles of logs to contain the soil. There is no compost or barn manure to spare, but when the horses are home, they forage in the park just outside the boundary fence. I collect their droppings, and those of the bears, and pack them home too. I plant tomatoes next to the porch and scarlet runners where they will grow up the south side of the house. The beans will benefit from this hot, sheltered location, and I will enjoy their shade when the sun is fierce at the end of summer. In other climates, I have often seen grapevines trained on a frame over an outside deck to form a bower: I will have a bean bower.

The soil is so lacking in structure that it retains little moisture. Every day through the long, dry summer, I haul bucket after bucket of water up the ladder from the river and dump it onto the plants. The tomatoes thrive, and the beans become a cascade of red flowers; but although the bees and hummingbirds work them ceaselessly, pushing aside the coiled spring at the centre of the flower to reach the nectar, the beans refuse to set: I harvest only eight before the frost gets them.

At last, I find time to get into the high country. Three mountains can be seen from the homestead. Walker's Dome is the dominant one across the river. Mount Ada faces it—Ada, so legend has it, is Walker's wife—although only its tip is visible to us over the east wall of the valley, and it cannot be seen at all from my house. Trumpeter Mountain sits above the lagoon at the head of Lonesome Lake. It is an insignificant bump, barely higher than the valley walls, but it reaches above the tree line and the Turners tell me that the view from there is superb. I will tackle this one first.

A rough trail leads up the mountain from behind the original Edwards homestead where Trudy was raised. It has not been used for years and is choked with windfall. I follow the ancient blazes and begin to climb. It is always a thrill when the land begins to fall away. Gaps in the forest show an ever-widening horizon and quell the discomfort of aching legs and clothes sodden with sweat and chilled by the wind. About halfway up, the trail reaches a great bluff known locally as de Gaulle's Nose; there, although shadow still fills the valley, I walk into sunshine. The Turners' place is a good thousand feet below me, and it looks surprisingly small and doll-like in the cool morning air. A trail of blue smoke issues from the little house. Jack will be cooking breakfast, and by the toylike barn, Trudy will be picking her way through the dewy grass to milk the cow. The small patch of cleared land looks insignificant in the forest's dark, furry tide. Behind it, Walker's Dome is now crowded in by a host of other peaks.

A discarded deer antler lies among the rocks at the top of the bluff. The bleached points have been nibbled by mice, and a scuff of green mould grows on one side. What curious structures they are, with their ivory feel and burnt-bone smell. What a vast amount of energy is expended in their continual growth.

For the next while, the forest closes its ranks again. The trail seems steep and endless. The top of each rise shows another one ahead, and the distance is a great deal more than it looked from below. Then suddenly, the next rise is bare, and beyond it is the summit.

I can see 50 miles in all directions. To the north, the rounded, volcanic Rainbow Mountains glow pink, and close to them is the distinctive sloping snow patch at the top of Mount Stupendous that overshadows Stuie. Farther west, the Hunlen lake chain curves through its plateau, and I trace the route through the mountains above it that my European Friend and I travelled two summers before.

A mile straight down is Lonesome Lake. Its dark waters are roughened by wind, and the minute dots of the Edwards homestead buildings are clustered at one end. Upriver, the Turners' property has lost all detail. Looking beyond it along the great slash of the valley, I can see four more slabs of water: Tenas Lake, Rainbow Lake, Elbow Lake and, finally, after the long swampy area where the horses are taken to graze, part of milky-green Knot Lake, 30 miles away. Mount Ada bulks to the south, and behind me is the official summit of Trumpeter Mountain, a mere swelling in a tawny sweep of grass, combed by the wind and streaked with slabs of snow.

It is bitterly cold. The breeze that is tempering the June heat in the bottom of the valley cuts like a knife here, and the snow slabs are as hard as iron. I am on a level with the clouds, and they race about me, sometimes reducing my world to a few yards and pelting my coat with dry pellets of snow. Then they rip apart and chase their shadows over the grass while the sun flashes through holes of piercing blue.

Away from the lookout point, the bite of the wind is lessened, and snow-melt splashes and gurgles through carpets of anemones and pale globeflowers. In a month, these meadows, at present so drab and sodden, will be a cascade of colour, a riot of red paintbrushes, blue lupins and yellow and purple daisies.

An hour or two is all that I have time for in this arctic world. It seems a shame to have to descend so soon after the long climb through the for-

est, but I have to return by nightfall to my endlessly thirsty garden.

I am a slave to my vegetables, and many expeditions have to be curtailed. A trip up Mount Ada, the third of the sentinels that guard the homestead, cannot be missed. But I can afford only one night away from home.

There is no trail, and it is quite steep in places; it is not difficult, however, to pack to the tree line, make an overnight camp and climb up to 8,000 feet the following morning. The summit is cut off from me by a crumbling, knife-edged ridge, but it is not much higher. From where I sit, I can see the country to the south, the view that has, until now, always been hidden from me, even when I climbed Walker's Dome. The sight is breathtaking. Tiers of icy walls march into the blue distance. Far above them soars 13,000-foot Mount Waddington, a summit of sheer-sided fingers poking from great, looped swaths of ice. Were it not there, I'm sure I could see all the way to Vancouver.

Between my place and Stuie is a four-day hike that takes in Hunlen Falls, then wanders for mile after mile through fabulous flower meadows, culminating at the top of Cariboo Mountain. From here, it is possible to overlook the two tiny, wriggling rivers in the Bella Coola Valley — and the bare, bald scars of the logging operations at Stuie.

Cariboo Mountain is a wonderful place to watch the sun drop into the Pacific. Once, during the carefree time before I had a house and garden, when I could indulge more freely my passion for the high country, I camped up there for a couple of days, without a tent, in dense cloud, trying unsuccessfully to keep dry under a rock. At the end of the second afternoon, my rather sorry little perch was transformed into a magical eyrie on the brink of an enchanted world. The fog dropped away to the tree line, a few hundred feet below; however, it rose and fell like the swell of an ocean, sometimes enfolding me again but always moving and occasionally erupting in slow, silent explosions that trailed into nothing. The dying sun suffused the seething mist with pink, and later, a full moon shone, white as bone, over the silent, mercurial sea.

In the morning, the fog was gone. The mountain peaks that, divorced from the land, had floated so impossibly high above the cloud now attached themselves to the valley; they had become ordinary again.

Already, the brief summer is coming to an end. The purple mist of asters along the fences shows that it is time to can the garden produce. Soon, quarts of round, green peas and chunky yellow wax beans rub shoulders with the dust-shrouded jars of meat I preserved in the spring. There are berries to harvest: red currants, which make excellent juice when crushed, and the small, wild, purple gooseberries, which make deliciously tart jams and pies. Guarded by a barrage of spines, they are painful to pick but well worth the loss of a little blood.

It has been another very dry summer. One sultry August day, I canoe down the lake and hike up Hunlen Creek into the bottom of the canyon, hoping to reach the foot of the falls. No water runs in the gullies where they cross the trail, but as I climb the glaring granite boulders, I soon meet it, splashing clean and clear over the white, speckled stones. Within an hour, I have plunged into the gloom of the canyon. Although it is low, the creek, which increases in volume with every step, still whirls giddily between fantastic heaps of boulders and shattered logs piled at unbelievable angles; its voice booms about its sunless prison. The creek becomes too wild to cross, and I creep along the north wall, ever aware of the gigantic jumbles of overhanging masonry. It looks as though one touch would send the whole lot crashing onto my head.

The falls are hidden by buttresses of rock until the last moment, but long before I reach them, billows of spray dance around me, driven by their own private storm. All the world is roaring, wet and very cold. The sky is far above, a jagged slash of blue between towering, black canyon walls. I round a slick, black pinnacle and can go no farther. The foot of the falls crashes into a hole in front of me—the spray is blinding, almost asphyxiating. I try to climb the pinnacle to get a better view, but my courage fails me on the wet rock. In a tiny patch of mud is a fresh goat track; one or two small plants, perpetually drenched and shaded, grow in crevices. I discover the largest and most delicious wild strawberries I have ever seen, ripe two months later than in the outside world.

The roaring water drives me back, down through the trapped, Tolkien landscape. Like the water, I leap from boulder to boulder through the eternal gloom and follow the creek as it erupts from the canyon and spreads and relaxes and slowly falls into the shimmering, sunlit stillness of the lake.

Chapter 20
The Art Show

Winter started early again this year. In the middle of November, the temperature dropped to minus 30 degrees F, and it stayed cold for about 10 days. My extra floor insulation has improved conditions in the house a little, but it is still not good enough. We've had no snow, and the unprotected ground has frozen so deeply that when the Turners attempt to dig a hole to bury poor old Lucky, who sickened and died, they find the soil as hard as iron to a depth of two feet. Plants with a shallow root system will not overwinter well.

It has become impractical to keep the hens. If I am away in summer, it is easy to provide enough food and water for them in advance, but during severe cold spells, their water needs replacing two or three times a day. As I am usually away for several days when I go to town, it is too much to expect of my neighbours. So when the birds quit laying, I apologize to them and wring their necks; I will arrange with the floatplane base at Nimpo to have a regular supply of eggs flown in with the swan grain.

To fetch the horses from their summer grazing at this time of year requires an overnight trip. The Turners usually go together, leaving me with the cows, but this time, Jack is suffering from a backache, so he stays home and I agree to go with Trudy. We want to avoid camping out in 30-below weather if possible, but a sudden warmth could bring rain and turn the

rocky trails to ice, stranding the horses. If left in the swamp all winter, they would starve or attempt to come home on their own and come to grief on the ice. So when the temperature rises to 5 degrees F and we hear, on the radio, of rain approaching the coast (we are generally 24 hours behind Vancouver), we set off. A thin powder of snow has roughened the ice on Tenas Lake, and travelling conditions are excellent. Above it, the trail plunges again through the forest and emerges at the much longer Rainbow Lake. I have not been this far before, and it is, as always, exciting to step out onto the flat, white surface of new territory where new bends beckon and the miles slowly unravel. The wind is still from the north and behind us; it drives the snow powder in little singing skeins across the ice.

We dump our gear where we will camp that night, then continue to Elbow Lake. A deep and twisted body of water, it cannot be trusted this early in the winter, so despite the severity of the cold, we stick to the trail. At the head of the lake are the windswept flats, covered with orange slough grass and scrubby willows, that are home to the horses for much of the year. We crash through the frost-brittle vegetation for some little while before we hear the bells and find the horses: black, chunky Star; fat, golden Nugget and the two colts; plain Bess with her inelegant black patches; and Tempest, a buckskin with a character to match her name. They are pleased to see us, and they nuzzle our pockets for treats.

We lead the horses back to camp and turn them loose on a small meadow. We spread our sleeping bags on the trail, which is not a good idea as there are still bear tracks about, but it is the only place flat enough to lie on. The daylight is fading, and we light a fierce, fir-bark fire. It contrasts with a night so thick and heavy, it seems that were it not for the supporting columns of surrounding trees, the darkness would fall about our heads. As the fire dies down, the darkness becomes transparent again. The bark throws off an intense heat, and dry pellets of snow patter unheeded onto our clothes.

Although the air is still cold in the valley, we have heard a wild southerly roaring across the treetops all day. By morning, it has scoured away the arctic air, and the temperature has risen to several degrees above freezing. It is not raining, but the warmth has licked the snow off the lakes. They are swimming with water and green as jade. The trees and rocks are so much colder than the air that they have turned hoary with frost. The lake is far too slippery for the horses, so we stay on the trail. In places, seepages have oozed and frozen and oozed again, until tremendous cascades of ice run hundreds of yards down the mountain. We have to cut new routes around these for the horses, but by noon, the animals are happily munching in the barn. They will stay around home until the ice goes off the trails in the spring.

I have never been so broke. Last year was a tough one financially; no sooner did a bit of money come in than it went to pay the most urgent debt. The Turners helped by lending me building supplies that they had on hand, and Katie and Dennis supported me with food and even clothing. I have never owed money before, not even with a credit card; although the debt is never more than a few dollars, I cannot seem to get rid of it. It is a constant worry. I hope to rectify this by mounting an art show in Salmon Arm, the town closest to where I lived before coming to Lonesome Lake. Now that I have so much more time, I have started painting again.

In the past two years, art has taken on a whole new meaning for me. My earliest paintings were acrylic representations of well-known landscapes, with the inevitable quota of old barns and historic buildings. I started selling such works when I lived in New Zealand, long before I came to Canada. I found them easy to do but not particularly satisfying. It seemed to me that people bought the pictures for the subject matter; they cared nothing for the skill or individual creative expression of the artist.

During my first winter at Stuie, I was given a book about an artist who is well known in Canada but whom, in my ignorance, I had not heard of. Tony Onley's watercolours were a revelation to me. Although they were perfectly recognizable as the blue- and green-grey mountains and seas of the West Coast, the pictures were not of the scenery but of the paint itself. The runs, the blurs, the hard and soft edges, the smooth and grainy textures and the relationship of all these things to each other: these were what made the paintings. Composition suddenly made sense. They looked so easy. All I had to do was switch from acrylics to watercolours and paint like Tony Onley, and I would be made.

Of course, my first attempts were disasters. Only great skill and experience can produce a seemingly effortless painting. But by the end of the winter, I had done much experimenting with different brushes and papers and had learned a lot about the way the minerals in the paints interacted with each other; I felt that I had made progress. During the following summer, I was too busy to paint, and it was not until last winter that I could tackle it again. It was then that I started to produce something that I liked. I still have an enormously long way to go, but at last I am excited about some of my work. Instead of the bright acrylics for which I used to be known, I now produce pale grey abstracts of the mountain shapes and clouds I see all around me.

Art shows are always a gamble, because it is impossible to predict the outcome. On the plus side, I am well known in Salmon Arm; although I have not visited there for three years, I still have a lot of friends, and people have been following my adventures through articles in the local newspaper and letters to CBC-Radio. Salmon Arm has an active and supportive arts council, which, along with my friends, has worked hard to publicize the show. But everyone is talking about a recession. And my supporters like scenery and old barns. How receptive will they be to my new paintings?

I want to drive the 700 miles, for I have a lot of paraphernalia, but to do that, I have to take the plunge and borrow yet more money, the rather daunting amount of $300, to pay for gas and insurance. The old truck is in a dilapidated state: it leaks a great deal of oil, and the exhaust system has disintegrated. To preserve my sanity as well as my hearing, I wear ear protectors when I drive.

It is a glorious day as I start up The Hill. Since my first trip on this highway, it has been widened, but it takes a lot of courage to inch close to the icy, unprotected drop to avoid an oncoming vehicle. Everything enters or leaves the valley by that hill; the ferry service up the coast has long since been discontinued, and the small planes that operate from the airport have very little space for freight. Despite its horrors, logging trucks, gas tankers and container trucks negotiate the road in all types of weather. The bus comes from the interior twice in seven days, the mail three times, and if the townspeople do not buy their milk and eggs between Thursday and Saturday, they might well have to do without for a week. Once, a slide blocked the road for 10 days, but it is rarely closed for more than a few hours; the highway crew do a great job of maintenance. A few people have gone off the edge of the road, but no one has been seriously injured.

From Heckman Pass at the top of The Hill, the road drops gently through the Chilcotin for 250 miles to Williams Lake, where it joins the highway network of the rest of the province. The threadbare carpet of lodgepole pine that covers the rolling hills of the Chilcotin is the result of an attempt to burn the whole country and turn it into grazing land. But there is too little moisture for grass to survive. The first tree to colonize after a fire is the pine. So much pine has matured all at once that huge areas have succumbed to waves of pinebark beetle, and in some areas, the dead standing trees are an enormous fire hazard.

I love that country—high, wide and cold and scattered with lonely ranches. The people who live there, 50, 60 or 100 miles apart, are my neighbours; although many of us have never met, we hear so much about each other that we can never be strangers.

I stay the night on a ranch; the following morning, as I drive through a Christmas-card world of brilliant sunshine and sparkling snow, fortified by what is reputed to be the strongest coffee in the Chilcotin, my heart is singing within me. Because of the ear protectors, I do not hear the telltale ticking of an engine starved of oil. The truck suddenly lurches and rapidly loses power. I can still move slowly, and I limp down the last hill into Williams Lake trailing clouds of blue smoke. The truck will need a new motor, and the repairs will cost $1,200. I am devastated.

Kind friends in Williams Lake put me and my mountains of equipment on the bus. As the miles roll by, I spend a sleepless night wondering about my future. My debts loom enormously. How will I ever cope with them? Will the truck ever run again? Perhaps I will have to try to find work outside, but where? There are precious few jobs in the valley, and I would simply go crazy in a city. Out here, in this alien environment, I am gripped by outside forces I cannot control. I feel I am being rushed to the brink of a bottomless chasm from which there is no turning back. I can do nothing but ride with the current and trust to fate.

It is only when I travel to a city that I become aware of the way in which most people live. My first reactions are to the speed and the smells, particularly car exhaust and cigarettes, and I am overwhelmed by the noise. Electric houses hum and furnaces roar. Televisions and radios slam out gossip and jingles in a bewildering manner, and each competes with the other for loudness and sensation. It is sad to think that most people are so numbed by it that they no longer hear it.

Artificial light glares off artificial surfaces. Everything seems so shallow. As a child, I frequently watched my father stain, then French-polish a table. After days of work, the shine was so deep, it seemed as though I would fall into it. Factory furniture has a different finish. The stain and polish are sprayed on in one coat, like the thin veneer of our society — one scratch shows shoddy and inferior materials underneath.

People call my home remote, but when buildings and vehicles are so superheated that it is possible to live one's whole life without setting foot out of doors, it is the people in them who are remote, because it is they who are out of touch with the world. They no longer need take responsibility for their own warmth, food, shelter or entertainment. It is they who have isolated themselves by erecting barriers against reality.

We are due to open the show on the Friday night, and my apprehension grows as we add the final touches to the display. At 7:30 p.m., we unfasten the door. There is already a group of people standing outside. It is wonderful to see so many old friends. That evening, and for the subsequent two days of the show, there is a constant stream of visitors. It is enormously gratifying to watch their favourable reactions to the paintings. They exclaim, they stay, and they come again with their friends. To add cream to the pudding, they bring their chequebooks. The money pours in. It will be spent instantly on debts and urgently needed food, art supplies and winter clothing. Nothing will be left, but at least I can live for the next few months. It's amazing how money always seems to turn up when it is most needed. The show has been an unprecedented success.

I get a ride back to Williams Lake, but as it will still take several days to fix the truck, I catch the twice-a-week local bus back to Stuie. This is no slick Greyhound, but the old, green converted school bus with its permanently rock-scarred windshield is more than just a vehicle. It is an institution that provides a lifeline through the scattered communities of the Chilcotin. Passengers are few, and part of the back of the bus has been walled off for freight. The driver has owned it for 13 years and knows absolutely everyone.

It is cold on the Chilcotin, with temperatures down to minus 13 degrees F. At Nimpo Lake, two hours before Stuie, the bus's alternator packs up, and there is no power to spare for the heater. It is pointless to discontinue the journey, for there is no replacement vehicle, but everyone is warmly dressed and cheerfully accepts it as just one of those things.

So as my goods are dropped by the roadside in the freezing dark and the passengers chorus "good-bye" from the black and lightless interior of the bus, I feel that my reentry into the valley is triumphant. For two weeks, I have been treated like royalty, praised, fed gourmet meals and chauffeured everywhere. But already, the skin of the outside world is falling away, and in my mind's eye, I can see the yellow log walls, the calm circle of lamplight, the silent, frozen forest and the brilliant night sky undimmed by city lights. I will be glad to be home.

Chapter 21

Winter of the Wolves

November was all the winter we had. January has been so mild that the temperature never once dropped below freezing; all the meat that was butchered at Christmas had to be canned within three weeks. I shall always remember this as the winter of the wolves.

One morning in December, the dog barks. The bears have been late going to bed in the mild weather, and the occasional grizzly is still travelling upriver, leaving such clear tracks in the snow that all the little wrinkles of skin on the underside of its paws are sharply defined. I look out of the window, hoping to see the bear. At the edge of the clearing, about 30 yards behind the house, the dark shape of a dog frisks about. Only it isn't a dog: it is a large, black wolf. There are more among the trees. The forest is alive with them, running and weaving back and forth; I count 10, although there may be more. Half of them are black, and the rest are so pale that they flicker like ghosts between the heavy, dark trunks of the firs. They seem amiable, with pricked ears and wagging tails, and are obviously interested in making friends with the dog. But she retires under the house. She has made the right decision, for there are many stories of wolves luring a dog to their pack, then killing it.

The pack moves into the forest and begins to yip and howl, a deafening chorus at such close quarters. I make the mistake of grabbing my camera and rushing outside. The howling stops. The closest wolf gives one deep bark, and they all simply melt away. One moment the forest flowed with movement, the next there is nothing. I become aware of very cold feet. In my excitement, I have forgotten my boots, and I am standing in the snow in my socks.

Just before Christmas, I see the wolves again. I have booked a plane to bring in groceries, and two days before it is due, I hike down to the lake to make sure the ice is thick enough for the plane to land on. I step from the purple-shadowed trail into the sunshine of the lagoon, and as the dog begins to run across the lake, nose down to the smells, there is another deep bark. The wolves are a few yards up the side of the mountain, and this time, they are much more reluctant to depart.

It is one thing to look at such creatures from the security of solid log walls but quite another to stand unprotected in the middle of a frozen lake. Although I know from statistics that the wolves will not attack, their blood-curdling howls and moans are alarming; it is impossible not to feel fear. But the wolves are friendly, whining and wagging their tails, and they do not leave the trees. Slowly, they draw back, and I hear their singing receding up the mountain. The reason for their reluctance to leave immediately becomes obvious. Several ravens, who are cawing and flying in circles overhead, dive downward and emerge squabbling and crashing through the branches, trailing ragged red strips of meat from their beaks. I keep the dog away from the kill and hope the wolves will return.

When I meet the plane two days later, there is no sound from the hillside, and I follow the wolf tracks up through the windfalls. There is little left of the deer: only a few hairs, the silagelike stomach contents and a patch of blood-stained snow. Of skin and bone, there is not a trace.

My third encounter with the wolves is in the new year. I am taking part in the Federation of Naturalists' annual bird count (all interested persons in a community agree to count together on a day close to Christmas, but as I am the only one in my area doing it, I can be more flexible). I spurn the trail and follow the braided channels of the river above the homestead, heading upstream and looking for dippers. After a couple of hours of puttering and following the vagaries of the river, I reach Tenas Lake. The flat, sunlit expanse is blinding after the close shadows of the forest. The wolves are quite clear, about a mile away, lying on the ice. Once again, there are 10 of them. They are aware of me at once. Several jump up and run for the nearby mountain, but three begin to cross the lake. It is about a mile wide just there, and the wolves stop several times and bark and howl in a rather disgruntled manner—not the sort of silvery singing that carries so far on a still night but a trapped howling, like that of a chained dog. Once off the ice, they seem to be coming toward me. I eye a tree, for I would love to climb it and wait to see what the wolves will do, but the dog would be left undefended on the ground. Perhaps my dipper count is not so important after all. I retreat into the forest, and the wolves do not follow. Later, I find their tracks leading out of the valley.

They are gone for several weeks, but then they sing again, and I see the remains of several kills. Early one morning, when I am walking down the ice of Lonesome Lake, I find a partially eaten deer. An eagle and two ravens are busy with the red rib cage, but they fly off as the dog approaches. Although the dog is very interested in the carcass, the fresh wolf smell must scare her off, for she will not touch the meat. As we stand and look, a long moan floats down the mountain. A few days later, when I return that way, the kill is gone and the wolves with it. I never see them again.

During the winter, I often meet a mother moose and her two calves. When they disappear during the reign of the wolves, I fear the worst. But just before the snow melts and the wolves split into small groups and pairs to have their young, the moose and her calves are back again, feeding unconcernedly in the willows while I watch them from the canoe in the river, barely a paddle length away. Frost rims their ears and the long fringes of mane along their necks. When the snow melts and the deer come down from the sunny ridges in groups to feed on the new growth as they always do, there seem to be just as many as ever. They stare, bat-eared, from the dun, deer-coloured forest or bound away, white-rumped and stiff-legged, like horses on a merry-go-round.

The longer days bring the usual restlessness, and they drive me from the confines of the valley to the top of Trumpeter Mountain. Walker's Dome has a predawn glow as I strap snowshoes to my pack; a couple of hours later, I stand in sunshine on the top of de Gaulle's Nose. A profusion of split hoofprints and depressions in the old, hard snow show where the deer have rested—this is where I found the antler on my first trip up here. A little higher, and the snow deepens quite suddenly. I lace the snowshoes to my boots. The way is steep, and the foot of powder slides uneasily over the icy mass underneath. My feet slip with it. I am constantly having to extricate my arms from shoulder-deep drifts; the more I push with my hands, the deeper I sink. Six plodding steps, a fall, a rest and six more steps. Will I ever make it?

Higher up, where the trees become scattered and stunted, the snow is thick and as smooth as whipped cream. There is little sign of life, but twice, hare tracks brush the surface of the snow, and once, a blue grouse, plump as a chicken, flies heavily onto a low branch, peering at me suspiciously from beneath its arched red eyebrow. From far below, I hear the faint bugling of the swans increase to a babble of sound; then there is silence, and I know they are being fed.

The blazes on the trees are buried, but the route is not hard to find, and after six long hours, the bare summit ridge is in front of me. It has been scoured down to rock by the wind, and a great cornice hangs over the edge. An overcast sky has chilled the day, and the encircling panorama of silent peaks is blank and white against a clay-coloured sky. When I first came up here, the surrounding mountains were an alien confusion of rock and ice. Now their shapes are familiar, and as I climb, they pop up like old friends: the Rainbows, Stupendous, Cariboo Mountain, Eagle Beak, Mount Talchako, Walker's Dome, Mount Ada and Monarch. I have walked their windy ridges, slept in their hidden valleys and drunk from their shining streams.

Lonesome Lake is grey. The ice is beginning to disintegrate, but the Hunlen chain, over 2,500 feet higher, lies diamond-white in its dark blanket of forest. A thin mountain wind moans over the cornice, and two small black eagles swing in wide spirals far below. How swiftly they can fly the distance it took me so long to travel.

It is too cold to linger long, and besides, time is pressing, for the days are still short. Going down is much easier. I skate through the loose surface snow until I reach the bluff. The wind has risen, and it is beginning to break up the overcast sky. A bronze sun breaks through a brassy slash, and I stop and melt snow for tea. The wind whips the flames of the little fire to rags; the ball of the sun burns its way toward the sea. The homestead, shut in by the walls of the valley, has long been in shadow; I have a feeling of claustrophobia at the thought of exchanging my airy perch for the darkening forest. But as I drop wearily down toward the dusk, I take with me the feel of the wind and clouds. It comforts me to know that the mountain will always be there.

Chapter 22

A Photographic Journal

I t is hard to conceive of living by oneself, 27 miles from the nearest road, 95 miles from the closest store; harder still to imagine falling trees and fashioning a house to withstand the seasons. Perhaps it takes a photograph to convey the magnificent allure of the landscape and the brute physical reality of making one's place in it.

In an odd way, the photographs reproduced here make the house-building project seem almost ordinary. Cutting notches, raising walls, milling lumber in a construction site strewn with butt ends and chain saws: this is standard log construction. It is easy to forget that there is only one other house within miles of the cabin at singing river, that it sits in a river valley 100 miles inland from Bella Coola, buried near the eastern edge of Tweedsmuir Provincial Park, a day's hike from chainsaw repair shops and fuel depots. All the more surprising, then, that this is not a ramshackle hermit's cabin but a 900-square-foot L-shaped bungalow with a deck and a loft.

Beyond that cabin stretches true wilderness, where one can step on stones that have never felt a human foot and see, for the very first time, a crisp glacial lake. The photographs have not been framed to exclude the tourist town at the base of the hill or the hydro towers looming in the distance. This is true wilderness, virtually untouched and untainted.

Page 137: When the ice melts on Lonesome Lake, bottom, the gear is flown in, then horse-packed to the camp, top, set up downriver out of the way of falling trees. The buckets of food, racks of utensils and rusty camp stove are fenced in against curious cows.

Page 138: Through the first summer, the walls of the cabin rise slowly, bottom. At the corners, the logs must be notched to fit snugly together. First, a rough notch is shaped by slicing into the log at one-inch intervals, the wood knocked out with a three-pound hammer, top left. Then the log is flipped, the notch rescribed and an exact fit carved out with the chain saw. An Alaskan Mill, top right, ripped logs into rough-cut lumber for window and door frames, floor planking and primitive furniture.

Page 139: With the help of neighbours Jack Turner (right) and Isabel Edwards (left), the pole that will form the ridge of the roof is hauled up with block and tackle and secured to the king post.

Page 140: The house is essentially a 28-by-26-foot rectangle with an 8-by-13-foot notch cut out of the one corner. The roof is cut away on the southwest side, but the four foundation logs extend fully, top, to create the basis for a deck with a view of the river and the setting sun. Scheduled to take a couple of weeks, building the roof drags on for months, bottom. It is unnerving working so high off the ground, fetching dropped tools takes precious time, and fitting the pole rafters to the log walls is painstaking work.

Page 141: Grizzlies prompt an early transfer from the campsite to the uncompleted house. By winter, an outhouse and a chicken house are added to the clearing and some alders cut back to allow an unobstructed view of the river, top. Inside, the cabin becomes more civilized, bottom, as rough-cut lumber becomes shelves, bookcases and window trim.

Page 142: After the monthly mail trip to Nimpo Lake, the 27-mile hike home begins on a trail leading to Hunlen Falls lookout, from which Lonesome Lake can be seen twisting southward toward the Atnarko—the singing river, top. Summer in the mountains brings a palette of wildflowers—valerian, senecio and paintbrush, bottom.

Page 143: With the house built, there is time to explore the slopes and valleys of the Coast Range. Directly across the river rises Walker's Dome, top, the highest of three mountains that cradle the homestead. At every turn lie breathtaking views—abstract sweeps of black rock and blinding snow broken by ultramarine lakes like Ptarmigan, bottom.

Page 144: People from the city wonder how those who live in the bush survive without laid-on entertainment. But even in winter, the land is rarely still. Martens, wolves and moose share the river with the settlers, top. Lonesome Lake is especially famous for its trumpeter swans, bottom, a flock of 400 birds that winters on the lake, sustained by a government feeding programme.

Epilogue

The house is empty now. The roof will probably succumb to the heavy winter snowfalls, but the walls are strong, and they will stand long after the forest has claimed its own. No human eyes look through the windows at the river running past the door; the grizzly walks his ancient trails in peace.

But that house is part of me. I still see the logs, which I raised with so much anguish: I remember each one, the problems it gave me and the place where once it grew.

And I can see the wolves, frisking in the yard and running, ever running, through the forest; and I feel again the wonder as the flame-red salmon sway across the gravel bars. I can see the swans, pounding their feet upon the drum skin of the ice, beating time to their age-old melody as they wing their way into the orange dusk; I can hear their mournful calling as they bring the winter with them from the north. I can smell the scent of summer flowers blooming in the meadows, and once more, I climb the mountains and stand above the eagles while my spirit soars to the heavens and the world swings away from my feet. My mind still sings with the thin, high wind and spirals with the eagles in ever-widening circles over the vast and endless wilderness.

Editor's Note

Chris Czajkowski no longer calls the cabin on the singing river home. She now lives 40 miles southeast of Lonesome Lake and 10 miles outside of the southern boundary of Tweedsmuir Provincial Park on the shores of a 5,000-foot-high, fly-in lake that is surrounded by mountains. She has built two cabins there, this time completely on her own (see *Harrowsmith* Number 87). From the cabins, she operates the Nuk Tessli Alpine Experience, an opportunity for artists, hikers and naturalists to discover the beauties of the Coast Range. She can be contacted by writing to The Nuk Tessli Alpine Experience, Nimpo Lake, British Columbia V0L 1R0, Canada.

Jack and Trudy Turner have also left Lonesome Lake; they recently moved down the valley to be near their daughter, now married, and their grandson. Their homestead has been purchased by Tweedsmuir Provincial Park and will be allowed to return to wilderness, together with Chris's cabin.

The Edwards family, of which Jack and Trudy are a part, have an interesting story. Those who would like further information about them and the Lonesome Lake area should consult *Crusoe of Lonesome Lake*, by Leland Stowe (Random House, 1956); *Ralph Edwards of Lonesome Lake*, by Ed Gould (Hancock House, 1979); *Fogswamp*, by Trudy Turner and Ruth M. McVeigh (Hancock House, 1980); *Ruffles on My Longjohns*, by Isabel Edwards (Hancock House, 1980); *The Story of Lonesome Lake*, video by John Edwards, Bella Coola, British Columbia, Canada (available from the artist).